The Brightes

The brightest star in our night sky is the blue-white Sirius known as the Dog Star. Each year it appears on the horizon behind our Sun with such exact timing that the ancient Time Keeper races, the Egyptians and Mayans, calculated their planetary year cycle by its heliacal rising. First appearing on July 26 at the start of Mayan calendar, the star would align with the Egyptian Giza Pyramid complex on August 8, celebrated as the Lion's Gate, before completing its yearly cycle of supreme influence on August 12.

Sirius has long been seen as a guiding light and the main evolutionary force for our planet. The Egyptian hieroglyphs link the god beings of Osiris and Isis with that star. Many of these ancient cultures believed in its capacity to accelerate consciousness through its yearly influx of evolutionary light codes channelled through our sun.

To connect with the energy of this beautiful star as it completes its yearly visit, is to open our consciousness to receive these galactic codes of light, and so accelerate our own awakening and assist the evolution of humanity.

In 1862, a companion star, Sirius B, was discovered by astronomer A.G Clark but the Sudanese (Dogon) had always believed that it is a triple star system with a larger dwarf star, Sirius C, that has a planet revolving around it that many of us originally came from.

Greg Branson, when aged 5, pointed that star out to his mother and said, "I came from there." He now knows that this was some twelve thousand years ago into the nascent Lemurian civilisation. His exciting new autobiography, "We are Sirians" charts his journey through the 28 subsequent lives that he has lived on Earth since then.

WE ARE SIRIANS

A Spiritual Odyssey for our time

by Greg Branson

Filament Publishing

Published by
Filament Publishing Ltd
14, Croydon Road, Beddington,
Croydon, Surrey CR0 4PA UK

+44(0)20 8688 2598
www.filamentpublishing.com

We are Sirians - Greg Branson
© 2023 Greg Branson

ISBN 978-1-915465-17-7

The right of Greg Branson to be identified as the author of this work has been asserted by him in accordance with the Designs and Copyrights Act of 1988 Section 77

All rights reserved
No portion of this work may be copied in any way without the prior written permission of the publisher

About the Author

Greg Branson moved from Australia to London in 1973 where he realised immediately that he had to develop as a healer and trance medium. His early training was with Ivy Northage at the College of Psychic Studies, and later with the fine channel, Maisie Besant.

During this period of great change and much turbulence, many spiritual leaders with special abilities beavered away quietly out of the public eye, establishing a network of small and vital healing initiatives that awakened people to the subtle realms.

Greg has done little public work, preferring to focus his abilities into developing the Helios Centre, a holistic healing charity which looks after people with mental and physical illness.

He started Helios in one room on Warren Street in 1976, which subsequently occupied a number of venues including a grand Nash house on a ley line opposite Regents Park. In 1992, they settled in Kings Cross.

Greg's highly innovative spiritual work has been carried out through the Maisie Besant Foundation and he has quietly channelled practical spiritual philosophy for the benefit of small groups of dedicated seekers since then.

He teaches his students to focus the mind precisely, so that the Aquarian energies of transformation are harnessed and directed into people with physical or emotional infirmities with such precision that the cause of their afflictions can be unlocked and resolved.

A true visionary, Greg is able to perceive the higher worlds with exceptional clarity and he can delve deeply into the realms of inner Earth to work with the beings who live there. His pioneering work ensures that the relentless shadow forces cannot undermine the achievements of those good souls at the forefront of social and spiritual change.

Greg is also a spiritual trouble-shooter working with his group, The Peacemakers', to clear blocked karmic energies at important sites in the United States, Australia and Europe and they have, especially, rejuvenated many major power points around Britain.

Most of these sites resonate with earlier eras but the entrances to the highest available energy have been displaced to secret points nearby, so that they can be worked on by those with the ability to do this. Cadbury Castle, near Glastonbury, is one such place and Bodmin Moor is another.

Greg's understanding of past lives is second to none. He works in a very flexible and intuitive way because all clients are different with complex past patterns that require very precise ways to deal with them.

His book 'Serial Consciousness' is a required text for this. Greg also runs 'True Ability' workshops with Robin Baldock and their 'Enlightenment for All' workshops enable participants to reach an exact energy balance so that they can open up directly to their own soul consciousness.

Truth is many-layered and spiritual seekers uncover each level only when they are ready. In writing his fascinating life story, 'We are Sirians', Greg has woven his profound conceptual understanding, that is often provocative and rarely comfortable, into a form that will help many to go deeper. It is time for his vision and methods to be more widely available.

Alhena
Meissa
Gomeisa
Minor
Procyon
Betelgeuse
Bellatrix
Orion
Mintaka
Alnitak
Alnilam
Monoceros
Trapezium
Cursa
Saiph
Rigel
Sirius
Mirzam
Arneb
Lepus
Nihal
Canis Major
Wezen
Adhara
Aludra
Furud
Columba
Phact

Table of Contents

1. Early contact with the stars — 11

    1943 — 18
    1948 — 23
    1953 — 23

2. Touching down — 28

3. Home is where the heart should be — 43

4. Love is all there is — 56

    1975 — 65

5. I meet my guides — 72

    1976 — 84

6 The Glastonbuy adventure — 89

    1977 — 89
    1978 — 99
    1979 — 100

7. When the Dark and Light embrace — 105
    1981` — 105
    1987 — 107

8 Achieving balance at last — 118

    1989 — 119
    1990 — 121

9. Our Egyptian adventure — 134

    1995 — 134
    2002 — 147

10. The final visits to Egypt

    2003 — 149

11 The return to Lemuria — 164

    2005 — 164
    2006 — 171
    The Second Visit — 178

12 Atlantis at Last — 185

    2012 — 185
    2013 — 193

Syrian Timeline — 194

13. The Atlantean Triangle — 197

    2014 — 203

14. Leaving Lemuria — 206

    2015 — 206

15, Beast of Bodmin Moor — 216

    2016 — 216

16. The Arthur ~ Marlin triange — 224

    2018 — 224

Chronology — 238

1
Early contact with the stars

On my not particularly welcome 80th birthday, I was invaded by a rare despondency on waking suddenly from a deep sleep. Flashes of memory intruded then, fearful scenes setting off wild heart palpitations that just getting on with life had always kept at bay. I was a frightened boy again.

Then figures from my past emerged, reaching out to me. First up was my much loved maternal grandmother, very alive, and joined by her loyal maid, Louie, who looked after me on the many occasions when my parents had more important things to do. I thanked them both and with a rueful smile wondered what would have happened if those two devoted women had not been there for me.

Ma wagged her finger sternly as she repeated her mantra, "Keep going, laddie. Always help your family and your friends, smile a lot and never give up. That's the way to outpace the devil." I opened my eyes and they were gone. Then as other, less happy recollections began to dive in, I whipped them shut again with a spitting, "Enough of that!" and, breathing deeply, lay back and waited for my friend, Satan, to catch up.

"Stop", he called out to me, as he always has, "Stop avoiding your past."

"Sod off, Satan. I know what you're up to," I shouted. "You're wasting your time. I know what my life is about now, no thanks to you," heard by the insomniac guy in the flat above who responded appropriately.

Then I listened intently, expecting to hear from the wise ones in spirit that I could usually rely on to keep this pesky intruder out but no, he kept on insisting, "Stop avoiding me! There is much more to remember."

At my advanced age, nothing much matters in the greater scheme of things, yet a lingering sadness reminded me that everything matters far more with so few years left to complete my mission. As thought can't be controlled indefinitely, I gave memory full rein and succumbed to the awfulness of regret.

Tears streamed out from a backlog of grief and disappointment at a life that had not lived up to the high expectations I'd placed on it. I went back to my younger days and saw that, no matter how hard I tried, I felt totally unworthy to be my father's son and follow in his increasingly successful footsteps. So, I held back the kind of assertive behaviour that would make me the astute businessman and versatile sportsman he wanted me to be.

When the tear gush at last subsided, I practised what I teach. After slowing down my breathing, extending the outbreath and shaking out a few of the remaining resistances, I reached a still place in my heart. Though peacefully detached, and without thoughts, I remained vividly aware.

Surprisingly, I needed to coax myself to revisit some more recent spiritual awakenings, sudden moments of clarity that had caused me to change direction and hone my emerging philosophy through a series of inner explorations with unexpected conclusions. Then, I remembered some outer journeys that took me far away from the false lifestyle that the world wanted me to cultivate. To keep going, I built up a firm unshakeable belief, that I could, should, would make a real difference in this world.

Yet, of the themes zig-zagging through my mind, the most vivid was the deep underlying frustration, I have long felt, that humanity is just not moving forward fast enough, and we are wasting our time on distractions and cruel repetitions of old errors. In many past lives, on exposing the obscenities perpetrated by those in high authority, who thought they knew better than the creator, I came a cropper every time. Now, I'll just have to live with their immaturity and be patient.

Thoughts of the day ahead stopped any further recriminations and I laughed at Satan clutching ineffectually, unable to get a grip on my slippery aura.

It seems that old slave driver, Father Time, has granted me a few extra years to continue my exploration of other realms and complete the work I am doing with the band of extra-terrestrial immigrants who are moving our Western civilization forward.

In the shower, I decided to present the more significant planks of my still unfolding belief structure in book form so that members of my spirit family, which may well include you, can learn more about our shared destiny on this planet and future plans. I hope that my understanding and conclusions will be of some value to you.

At the computer now, I am allowing in vivid memories of events I had not appreciated at the time, showing how my troubled early years and the immaturity of my adolescent life, that stretched well into my twenties, linked directly back to many pockets of crucial experience in former existences. To see how and why the persistent errors inherited into the earlier stages of my present Earth journey, dovetail into those made and repeated by humankind across the ages.

I am starting to arrange my adventures in this life linking them to the other 32 incarnations on this planet that I know about, plus experiences in other galaxies and dimensions far from this, in order to complete this record and make some sense of the divine purpose behind it all.

As I type, I am trying to stop further intrusions from my meddling mind as the misty past swirls around with flashes of clear memory coming in, fragmented at first, but gradually becoming a lucid cavalcade of linked episodes, inter-relating, interweaving, absorbing each other's vital energies, all appearing to be still happening,

I must slough off yet more mental interventions, the many doubts and recriminations I cling on to, before an extended segment pulses forward and there he is. How old? Eighteen – shortly before leaving home to go to uni. Mum, at first a vague figure, gradually becomes more convincingly present. She is talking to him but, behind the smiles, there is a resentment that he had caused her so much pain as she struggled to understand his unusual nature and fulfil her parental duty to him.

She stresses that, in his early years, he'd been a normal happy boy caught up in the intriguing world of frogs and tadpoles in the creek down the road and playing with Tinker, a rebellious Australian terrier, with sharp, no-nonsense eyes, who cuddled up to him in ways she never did, his only real friend. Together, they shared many secret adventures. "What", she seems to be asking, "went wrong then?"

It was probably their decision not to have a second child, a daughter it would have been, that left him isolated and open to the influence of other worlds. He often visits inner places that his parents certainly know nothing about. He has learnt not to trust them to respond sensitively to what he is going through, especially when his imaginings take on a sinister tone. They would have worried for his well being even more than they did.

Despite living in an undistinguished suburb in the Adelaide foothills, this is actually a rather privileged family. Their modest house has a large backyard with lots of trees and shrubs that young Greg can disappear into when it suits him, and a double garage which is rare.

I have done a lot of focused introspective work in my adult years, delving back to the essence of being and I've regularly released the blocked energies from past lives energetically through my body, without always knowing where they came from, relying on this to keep me stable. I'd kept right away from the very early memories which were far more traumatic than I wanted them to be, but one is rising up now, demanding full attention.

That young boy is excitedly running around the garden and rolling on the lawn, with Tinker licking his face, just a few months after he turned four. Dad works for his "mean and nasty" father-in-law in the family business and is paid nowhere near enough to live comfortably. Yet they find the cash for mum to take him every morning to Mrs Colquhoun's kindergarten, to mix with other children who soon become willing players in his fantasy life of wondrous beings coming to earth to help them escape into a magical world beyond the reach of parents.

I can see the fabulous stairs leading up to her attic room. Each day, the children judged as being on their very best behaviour are allowed to go up and find a special sweetie on one of the steps. The higher up this treat is placed, the nearer to the angel woman he tells them lives in that room. He often imagines her golden hair, sylphan features and beautiful doe eyes.

He wants so much to meet her and, one day, standing at the foot of the stairs alone, he notices a light shining from the half-open door up there. She is waiting for him, surely. He musters the courage to climb the steep steps to visit his fabulous creation but, just before reaching the door, a voice intercepts. "What are you doing up there?" It is Mrs Colquhoun, looking very stern, "Only the very best boys are allowed to go that high." He'd always believed that he was one of her favourites, so his surprise plummets into deep shame.

Later that evening, he is lying down on the back lawn, scanning the sky. He picks out his first star and then another above the gum tree, and one more, a little fainter, too many by now to count. On which of these twinklers, he often wonders, does he truly belong?

Then, in a flash, his eyes fix on the brightest one, far to the right and, with no doubt at all, he points, "There it is!"

His father, a bookseller by day, brings home a picture book of the star systems known then. The young lad gazes at, then rejects each one until, on the final page, he is drawn to one star, by far the brightest. Surely this is it. He runs to his mother who tells him. "That's Sirus, dear, the Dog star" There is no doubt now. He came from Sirius.

Near the end of term at kindy, a concert has been planned. Young Greg is in his element and asks Ma to make him a costume as a star child. He doesn't hide his disappointment when it turns out more like an insignificant green elf. Stars shine. So, she adds a wand with glitter on a star-shaped mirror at the end.

The other kids are jealous, of course, mere earthlings in his eyes. There is no place in his cosmos for any rival star beings. The show is a marvellous success and he noticeably opens up with pride when surrounded by a gabble of mothers praising his performance.

The following evening, he takes mum into the back garden, pointing excitedly to his precious star. "I came from there", he exclaims, expecting a pat of approval, but all she manages is a "Don't be silly, dear" before packing him off to bed.

It was not the only blow she inflicts on my young self, undermining his self-belief and causing him to retreat even further from her conventional way of life. The next evening, father hands him a picture book on where babies come from. It doesn't get their anticipated response, for he knows better.

Every new person he meets is grilled, just in case they know what the others don't. He asks his Sunday School teacher whether his star is the one that the three wise men followed but her inevitable reply, that the only star that matters is the one that leads to Jesus, is hardly a useful response given His total indifference thus far.

Several months later, a second chance to visit the upper room presents itself. Young Greg is waiting for mum to pick him up after kindy but she's been held up. Mrs Colquhoun is on the phone to an agitated parent. He takes the first step up the stairs, heart beating, hardly breathing and he holds onto the banister, very tightly, in case he is discovered again and loses balance.

He pushes the door firmly at the bottom and it swings partially open. It is the spare attic bedroom used by Mrs Colquhoun's daughter when she returns home at holiday time, but now there is only a vast night sky stretching far beyond the figure of the star goddess he has come to meet. She is standing with her back to him, dressed in vivid purple. He climbs the remaining stairs and stands in the doorway, not moving. It is her space and he hasn't been invited.

Then she turns, very slowly, until he can see her luminous face with eyes that narrow into a laser-like intensity, a creature more vile than any he could have imagined. Her stare bores deep, shattering his expectations and precipitating sheer terror. He tumbles down the stairs and onto the floor at the bottom screaming hysterically.

He is being sucked down into the earth and has to hold on to a chair leg to stop it happening. I am empathising with his plight entirely and reliving the full horror of it.

Mrs Colquhoun is unable to stop the waves of tears and the shaking that is overwhelming him. When mother arrives, she is equally unable to calm him down. It is some hours before he quietens enough to be taken home.

At that moment, young Greg turns from a rather outgoing child to a shy, introverted one, furtively watching life happen and prone to sudden bursts of irrational fear in the early evenings. No one knows what to do with him. The desperate, "Help me. I'm frightened," directed towards the night sky, does little to relieve the situation. His star has abandoned him.

On overcast nights, he can make out shadowy figures in the clouds, skulking. They can't be angels. Angels have halos and beautiful shining faces. They must be friends of that devil guy, his Sunday school teacher so often warns him about. They are certainly unfriendly.

More involved now, I am aware of the grotesque intruders who are always lurking in the shadows once night falls. His bedroom is in the outside prefab extension on the other side of the rear porch. Every evening, after turning out the light to the main part of the house, he stands in the darkness, on the edge of fear, mustering the courage to walk very slowly, trepid step by trepid step, across the porch to the play area door, leading to his bedroom. When the light is turned on, the fear retreats.

Though his dog, Tinker, sleeps in the garage, and isn't there to support him through this nightly ordeal, he always reaches his destination safely. He could carry a torch but chooses not to. Always, before panic can take over, a strong, courageous presence comes to him, a guardian angel, if you like and, together, they are a match for the malevolent forces poised, waiting to overwhelm him.

Before retreating into sleep, mother always comes with a peeled and quartered apple. She kisses him on the forehead which is about as intimate as she ever manages. When she switches off the light, he knows that he will be safe if he pulls the bedclothes over his ears. Otherwise, he will surely be sucked down into the clutches of these monsters.

∞

1943

After a scorching January school holidays, my young self is enrolled at the local Rose Park primary school. The previous year, the Japanese bombed Darwin and their submarines attempted to enter Sydney Harbour. This is a long way off from Adelaide, but everyone is expecting this dreaded invasion to happen soon.

"The 'Japs' are coming to kill us," he is told and it might happen at any time. He won't have the chance to hide or escape to his true home in the sky which is now glazed over by the danger.

Every night, there is an eerie silence before a siren wails out its message, "Be afraid."

I am looking at the dreaded searchlights as they stalk the heavens, knowing that this 'enemy' has forced my young self to withdraw even more into himself. He can no longer sense his other world friends. Obviously, they have abandoned their positions close to him and retreated to somewhere safer.

It is weird. Each day arrives with his new teachers acting as if nothing is amiss and then, the night sky is filled with menace. In the schoolyard, the older kids, seeing his vulnerability, are taunting him with their "You'll be dead soon" abuse, as if they know what it really means.

Our parents aren't willing to discuss it with him. Their, "Don't worry, son. It will be all right," without a skerrick of explanation, is making the fear far worse.

Wedged between this present moment and those far back events, I am trying to identify with his undeveloped mind. Though there is little understanding of the adult world that he is forced to endure, his inner life is quite mature and adventurous. He has learnt to hold himself contained and very still so that nothing bad can get in. The ability, I now have, to confront so-called evil without flinching, was begun with his determination then that terror must never take over.

Inwardly focused, with breathing limited to short ins and outs, I am touching in on the horrific imaginings that he is managing to keep at bay. They include memories of battles experienced in former lives and the retreat to safety in underground caves.

There is no one around to confide in, though he does have fleeting visits from several friendly spirit beings.

When he asks them, "What does it mean?", the response is disappointing. "You will understand when you are older." Nevertheless, they are surrounding him with their love and me, as well. It is still needed.

That was quite a memory exercise. I am shaking my head to relieve the intensity of it. Moving on, I am now aware of a night, several years later, with a full wolf moon dominating the sky. A gloomy light is getting through the drawn blind enough for me to see that two of the monstrously deformed creatures, he often senses lurking around his bed, are actually taking form.

In the corner, grimly supporting them, I can see the woman who scared him so much at kindy. She is not in the slightest bit reformed. The wicked queen in Snow White was a softie by comparison.

He doesn't run to mother's bedside for comfort. There are no hugs and cuddles to be had there. He is shaking and sobbing so loudly that she comes anyway, watching from the doorway until the worst of his convulsions are over. Then she responds in the only way she knows how, by taking his hands and firmly repeating her mantra, "Be a man, my son."

I am sobbing almost uncontrollably now.

After a pause to blow my nose, I link up again with a "Good on you, mate," as he unexpectedly fights back.

"You don't understand. I don't need your help. Leave me alone," withdrawing again into his heart. They can't get at him there. It is his safe space but it isn't enough this time. Reinforcements are desperately needed.

Are his guardians around? No sign of them.

After an almost unbearable wait, I sense someone approaching his bed. Not one of the monsters, a benevolent being, it feels like. Suddenly, a light shines in, not with a strong intensity, more a coal-fire glow and it is coming from the floor.

We look over the side of the bed. There are stairs stretching down and a tall, bearded, wizard-like old man is climbing towards us. I feel an incredible relief as he approaches and puts his hand on the young lad's head. He has come, not from a distant star, but from within the earth to be our saviour.

From that moment, the underworld ceases to be a terror place for my young self. The intensity of his despair fades away and will not return. Before leaving, the old man gives a rather sad smile; probably because he knows what lies ahead. It will be a long time before he appears in person again but he will remain in the background to provide the comfort and inner guidance needed.

"Stay true to your beliefs, my son," is the message, "and you will become a man without anyone's help".

His parents are not bad people. They are doing their duty, but they have no idea of what he is going through. My young self feels much less vulnerable now and there is no more looking to the stars for support whenever faith falters, as it often does, in a world that remains a challenging place to be in.

༄

Next up, I am merging with another me, aged seven, sitting in my mother's wardrobe. I feel comfortable there and safe. Sometimes I put her clothes on.

Then, one sunny morning, I go round to the front door of our house, fully made up and wearing one of her outfits. I reach up, knock and wait, not really expecting what follows. For me, it's just a bit of fun.

Mum is not at all pleased to see me. Squeaking, squealing, she has no difficulty getting into a shocked mode and almost shouts, "What will the neighbours think?"

I hadn't thought of them. I turn towards the house next door and out comes a word I recently picked up at school, "Strewth!"

"And don't use words like that, ever. Never do that again. I am very hurt by your behaviour. I expected more of you." The big shock continues when I am grabbed and rushed indoors before anyone can catch sight of me dressed like a tart.

If you are now expecting an exploration of trans consciousness, don't. It is not something I would think of doing now but, then, I was being influenced by one of my very few female past lives, a courtesan.

&

The war is finally over and the sirens have stopped. None of the horrible events predicted actually happened but the relief, felt by everyone else, is only partial for my eight-year-old self. It will be quite a while before it is safe to look once again to the sky for answers.

Father enrols him at an all-boys private school, Prince Alfred College, his alma mater, a laid-back Methodist academy, certainly not as posh as St Peters, the Anglican college down the road but it provides respectable training for those wanting to get on in Adelaide society.

He is still mildly autistic, but his behaviour isn't at all irrational now. The adults in his life just see him as painfully shy. In reality, he is holding back, not feeling a part of this mysterious world. His few friends are all fellow outcasts.

His heart still withdraws slightly when darkness comes and the sky is overcast. Every evening, for several more years, he continues to act out his ritual of crossing the outside porch in the dark. He doesn't have to but he knows that it is a necessary part of his training to be strong in the face of unseen evil and, as I now see it, to venture into the darker places within the earth, where karma lies, and not be affected.

Young Greg is on a quest but he is still emotionally rather immature. He lacks the social skills needed to go beyond the isolation and profound loneliness that he feels God is asking him to bear. Nevertheless, he can muster undoubted courage and resilience when needed.

&

1948

Puberty arrives unannounced and the eleven-year-old me joins the local scout troop and eventually becomes a patrol leader. He always goes to the summer camp and sleeps out under the night sky whenever it is clear.

There, he confirms that the brightest star is his true home and he is on a mission to discover its secrets. He imagines happy people there, leading idyllic lifestyles and led by wise and upright men. He believes that he came in a spaceship looking for a better life and was forced to stay here even though he doesn't fit in. It is real science fiction stuff but some, I know now, was true memory.

He is also learning the most important lesson of all, to not let his shy human persona interfere with his courageous inner self. Acceptance of the hidden worlds is gradually developing along with the ability to relate to them imaginatively.

ે

1953

At age sixteen, the family moves house. I am experiencing his relief when all residual fear of the dark completely, almost magically, disappears. It will hold no dangers after that.

I enthusiastically start acting in school plays taking on the middle-aged female roles, never the glamorous young things. I am in my element, dressing up again and hiding behind a character, with my autistic tendencies nowhere to be seen. I deliver my lines confidently, haughty sometimes, a strong woman always and, I am told, rather outstanding in comedy roles.

While my love of playing someone else, liberates my deep unconscious, it appals my father, a conventional businessman who has begun what he hopes will become the largest publishing house in Australia, Rigby Ltd, producing locally written books. He is still expecting me to follow him into the business and carry his success forward, but this is not the way it is unfolding.

It is the sensitive, inwardly focussed Greg that I am empathising with now. He is holding back and merely observing the goings-on around while, at the same time, the other Greg alongside is managing to project a reasonably normal persona, attending school classes, playing sport, and tolerating the company of his boisterous schoolmates. Star gazing is put aside. There are exams to pass

On serious matters and when fear takes over, I have Mrs Dow to turn to, a big-hearted and very wise soul who runs the children's book department. She tells me that she has absolute faith that I will come through this ordeal and be very successful one day.

More memories are surfacing. There is "Tag", the maths teacher who rubs his willy against the boys' elbows as he leans over to check their sums, but not mine. How will I respond to that if he does? I'm not sure. And there is 'Tinny' Steele who uses the cane much too often, and beams as he counts the stokes, one, two, three... up to six for those especially naughty boys. I usually get three.

It is sad that the perverts and sadists are the ones standing out. There are plenty of decent chaps doing their best to inject interest into subjects of dubious value to me and the other C graders heading towards a career in minor management or expected to take over from dad on the family farm.

At last, I graduate to playing male roles, a villain in "The Fourth Wall", which means that father won't have to squirm with embarrassment, too much, when he comes to see me perform. In my final secondary school year, I am chosen to play Mr Bennett in Pride and Prejudice.

"Thank god for that", dad announces, "I don't want you doing any more of those pansy parts." However, fate plays a sneaky hand and the boy playing Mrs Bennett drops out. There is no one experienced enough to take his place. So, being very good at fluster and flounce, I succumb to the pressure being placed on me to switch roles.

I haven't the courage to tell dad until late in the rehearsals. His response is a silence that is certainly not golden. It glowers and accuses and condemns, but he knows that he can do nothing about it. The show must go on and it does, enthusiastically received by the audience except for that one seething critic who leaves straight after, taking the car and leaving mum and me to go home in a taxi.

For the entire month that follows, dad is incapable of speaking to me. When I come into the living room, he lowers his head and attends to the company accounts. I don't come in very often, staying many long hours alone in my room, grappling with my insecurities.

At Uni, I become the president of the dramatic society and can be found on stage more often than in the lecture theatres. I am rather good at being someone else, not so successful in the academic arena for I only just scrape by in enough subjects to remain enrolled.

I act in dozens of well-received productions, mostly in lead roles. Androcles is my most appreciated performance but my specialty is playing much older men. Petkoff in Shaw's "Arms and the Man," is the first and this continues for six years until the final night as Van Helsing, the famed vampire hunter. Immediately after driving the stake into Dracula's heart, I hear the words, "You will never tread the boards again." I stay in the profession, though, developing as a playwright.

I understand my parents' disappointment when I decide not to follow my father into the family business and, despite an urge to bring my unorthodox inclinations to the fore, I decide to maintain a respectable front, to please them. I become a secondary school mathematics teacher. My mother has already realized that I will never be happy in their conventional world and no longer introduces me to her friends' daughters.

Many of my own pals have embraced a bohemian lifestyle but I never go with them into the back alley venues they frequent or, indeed, much into their private worlds.

This sleepy city of churches and unquestioning conformity has its lower Hindley Street, where the bikers hang out. One Saturday night, after attending a film at a downtown cinema, I pluck up the courage to go there and talk to the night people but do not explore their world further. That will come later.

My fascination with the starry heavens slips into the background until 1964 when my teacher self puts a down payment on a tiny wartime prefab cottage perched on the side of a hill with a marvellous view of the city.

This is the perfect place to love and respect the earth. Many fruit trees are planted and I create a small open-air sanctuary, surrounded by a rock wall in which two large lizards take up residence.

Sleeping out there is essential on hot summer evenings. Sometimes, when waking in the night, I sense the two residents standing on either side of my head, as sentinels. I have many impressions of being with them in different forms and situations. A regular image is of two guards protecting the gates to an underground city. I implore them to let him through but before they do, sleep takes over again. In the morning, I know that I have been down there but can remember nothing.

Moving forward to my birthday on the 28th of November 1971, just before dawn. I can sense the lizards there wanting to communicate. A most unexpected message comes through from them. "To find the way back to your true home, you must first go to England."

My mind snaps back to a few years earlier when my good friend, John Rawsthorne, a very perceptive amateur palmist, read my destiny lines. "A long life", he assured me, "but you won't stay in Adelaide. You'll go overseas for quite a long time. Money will come to you eventually and you will be free to pursue a very unusual spiritual path."

He then studied the lines more closely with a magnifying glass before suddenly pointing, "Look there, below your little finger, that's the marriage line. It will happen in your early forties and you'll have a son. It's a bit confusing though. There is this other line, dividing it, see. It shows some kind of a split happening when you meet another person, later on, who is your true affinity."

That part didn't go down well at the time. I'm a loyal sort of chap. If you are wondering whether it actually happened, you'll have to wait, for this is the crux of my story and I don't want to spoil it for you.

Returning now to my teacher self, who is reacting to the news, from the lizards, that a trip to the mother country is imminent. A big step, but they do speak English there, so it should be all right.

Fortunately, three months long-service leave is due the following year. Travel from the end of the first school term in May is chosen to avoid the Australian winter. Sensible move that. Plans are enthusiastically made.

2
Touching down

Merging with my former self, I am clutching the armrests and forcing myself to breathe slowly as we drop through the swirling grey clouds above Heathrow airport on this particularly overcast day. While not exactly praying, I am craning my neck to make sure there is actually a runway down there and desperately hoping for a much-needed miracle to get us down safely.

It has been an especially bumpy trip, touching down briefly in Singapore, Bahrain and Rome for refuelling. All three airports were filled with armed soldiers, in response to various sieges and hijacks I've read about but don't really understand. In Rome, they all looked young and reckless, almost eager for the chance to shoot me dead.

The body search in Bahrain was much more thorough than actually necessary. My naiveté is fully exposed. I might have to convince him not to take me into a side room for a more intimate examination. He hints at this. As his fingers explore further up my leg, I assure him that my weapon fires only blanks. He quickly withdraws, looking intently into my eyes for a sign, then snorts himself into a smile. This is my first time away from Australia and my blinkered small-city reality. I am now facing a big wide world that seems anything but secure and user-friendly.

We touch down with a slight bump and an un-nerving veer. "Ooohh", then "oo-oo-oohhh" surges out of us, followed by the welcome back-thrust of the engines. We have made it. Everyone applauds the pilot enthusiastically, and I thank the cabin steward, whose risqué banter has successfully kept our minds off the precariousness of our situation. This Qantas flight has been great fun. It needed to be.

Still shaking a bit, I gratefully descend the stairs to the tarmac which is twinkling at me after earlier rain. The grey day matches the black and white Pathe newsreels that preceded the main feature at my local picture house back home and the terminal building looks reassuringly gaunt and historical though, of course, it isn't actually.

My initial toe-touch on to the mother country does not bring up the expected emotions. Instead, I'm suddenly aware that it is not just a brief long-service break from teaching mathematics and drama in the ultra-conservative education system back home in Adelaide. It now seems to be a perilous adventure without any guarantees that I will come through it safely.

I am being invaded by a confused mixture of strange impressions, high-pitched sounds and garbled voices. Though standing transfixed, I have no thought of bringing myself out of it. I have stepped into the back reaches of my heart which is familiar territory. As an actor on stage, I had always retreated there and let the character I was playing take over. But this is real life.

Suddenly the static clears and I am not alone now. Other-world beings are sharing my inner space and, though I can only sense them, they are very present and seem friendly enough.

I've not done drugs, except for one go on hash when, after fifteen minutes puffing away, I asked when it was going to begin. Clearly, I was not a natural for that. An Eden Hills high school teacher had experimented with LSD and tried to convince me to join him. From what the kids told me, I'm certain he took too much. Even if it was a far more exciting reality or un-reality he escaped into, I knew instinctively that it was not for me, and the reason is becoming clear now.

His descriptions of wild trips into other states of consciousness do not match what I am experiencing. I am not out of control or spacey. Nothing bizarre is taking over, well yes, it is a bit weird, but it doesn't actually seem so. I am entirely focussed within it.

I have often sensed a contact with these other world companions, apparently my life-long guardians, but they are much closer now and I am not questioning their invitation to join them on a "soul-transforming journey" into the unknown. There is a stark sense of inevitability about it all.

My previous spiritual search was confined to books and attending occasional lectures at the theosophical meeting house which were far too stuffy and arcane for my liking. A couple of Indian gurus had come to Adelaide but, other than two years as the only man in a hatha yoga class, I haven't been drawn much to the lotus position and the Eastern search for bliss. It seems far too indulgent and escapist for me.

I had been inspired by Anthony Borgia's 'Life in the world unseen', the channelled thoughts of Monsignor Robert Hugh Benson, a friend of the medium before he died, describing what it was like in the afterlife. A small Spiritualist movement in Adelaide did this sort of thing, but I chose not to attend their services. Yet, here I am, standing in a puddle, in direct contact with my own band of beings from beyond, telling me that I am about to set out on an unscheduled journey into other-world awesomeness with them.

The light is growing in intensity and I feel a tremendous expansion. I hope I don't burst. One of these spirits seems almost physically present. I reach out to touch him but a cautionary, "Not yet", begins my return to terra firma London.

A cold shiver tells me that there is no turning back. My rational mind fights to regain control. "This is ridiculous. Take no notice, You're only here for three months to see the sights, Big Ben and Buckingham Palace, like

Christopher Robin and Alice. You have a secure job back home." Checking. Yes, this is a return ticket.

So, what is this reluctance all about? I mean, I've successfully aborted an international assassination attempt at Rome Airport and fended off the unwelcome advances of a Bahrainian sex fiend. London should hold no terrors for me.

I certainly won't hit it off with the natives. That is a given. I served six years hard labour teaching mathematics in the satellite town of Elizabeth to mainly British migrants, leaving me in no doubt that the Anglo-Saxon English are not like me in any significant way. Yet, I know how to deal with them. I am prepared for their obstinacy, their thinly veiled sense of superiority, their inability to face challenges directly – though, just how impossible they are in their home environment, I have yet to discover.

So, with nothing to fear, why am I feeling desperately alone and abandoned? I can't even walk to the bus waiting to take us to the terminal. My legs won't budge. A concerned Antipodean hurries across to me.

"Is everything O.K?" I can only nod in response. She takes my arm and I walk rather unsteadily towards the bus. Yet, with every step, there is a mounting sense of relief.

I have actually taken the plunge and come this far, all on my own. Unbelievable! And to be welcomed by a group of advanced spirit beings inviting me to embark on a life-changing inter-dimensional escapade planned especially for me. I can only shake my head in eye-widening bewilderment.

I climb meekly into the bus to a chorus of "You all right, mate?", silently shamefaced and unable to make eye contact. From then on, after getting through customs without a hitch - Commonwealth citizens are still given favoured treatment - the day goes surprisingly smoothly. A slick train ride takes me to a small Kings Cross hotel booked for a few days by my cousin, Lynton, who runs the London end of the £10 pommie migrant scheme, till I get my bearings.

With my rational awareness fully reinstated, there is much to do. A reassuring trip to Australia House on the Strand is top priority followed by the move into a run down cheepie hostel to divert money for more important things. While somewhat excited by the prospect of this being also a supernatural adventure, I am more drawn to an exploration of the hidden places and unexpected pleasures to be found in the seedy side of Soho, that I'm reading about in the alternative guide book, which may need an altered consciousness to truly appreciate.

One opportunity appears when I am invited to a dead-of-night occult meeting where I have great difficulty in bowing down to their horned deity. This is certainly showing me what I must not get involved in. Creepy stuff.

A stern inner voice reminds me that I am here in London to investigate the authentic spiritual realms so, on the following afternoon, I dutifully approach the Spiritualist Association of Great Britain (SAGB), in their Belgrave Square headquarters, amid multifarious foreign embassies fronted by machine-gun toting guards, for an appointment to see one of their mediums.

This is the perfect place to re-contact my spirit inspirers. Emerging from the rotating front door into the grand entrance hall, there they are, occupying corners where shadows ought to be. There is one on the stairs leading to the conference rooms, morphing into others further up until there is a whole company of spirit beings beckoning me forward.

A tall imposing chap in religious garb approaches me. I try to look at him directly but can't. I can usually only see spirit beings at the sides of my awareness. So, turning my head slightly, that's better, I mentally ask him what he wants of me.

"We are here to support you."

"That isn't good enough. Be more specific," I snap back,

"Everything will be revealed in its own good time," is the unhelpful addition.

I am suddenly back in the entrance hall, rather dazed,

and wondering why I am here. Oh yes, a personal sitting with a medium. Perhaps some useful answers will come then. The reception desk woman gives me convincing evidence that she is a real person when she hands over a coupon and points towards a small side room where a friendly middle-aged woman is waiting.

"Oh, you are certainly one of us," is her opening line.

"Us?", I enquire, under my breath.

She doesn't hear this and continues, "You will be a healer and a humble teacher of the eternal mysteries of human existence." Not exactly the successful career in the theatre I am hoping to hear about.

"Your psychic abilities will be quite unusual, much more therapeutic than what I'm doing. But, before this, you must embark on a journey back in time to rescue fragments of yourself trapped there. Then you will find a doorway to the underworld and, on entering, you will encounter the deeper purpose to your life".

I am about to say, "That's bunkum," when I remember the lizards.

"But first", she firmly adds, "to be ready for this challenge, you must address your emotional blocks." She goes on to tell me about Quaesitor, a newly formed organisation promoting unusual new approaches to emotional and spiritual growth, facilitated by young group leaders brought over from America. I thank her profusely.

On weekdays, it is sightseeing and, at night, I attend as many theatre shows as I can afford but, she was right, at weekends, Quaesitor is the only place to be. Gestalt one week, bioenergetics the next.

"Why are you here?", the group leader usually asks.

"I want to find my true self", I reply, allowing myself to feel a bit exposed. I blush easily. It probably seems a bit pretentious.

When opening out my inner world to people I hardly know, I discover a secret store of unexpressed fears needing resolution and some really icky desires I would rather not come out. The big opportunity comes at the obligatory encounter group where we sit naked and let it all hang out. Courageously, I do not act on my intense wish to escape.

We go without sleep on Friday and Saturday nights to break down our inhibitions and barriers to spontaneous expression, to "access the deeper reaches of our fears and dreams", according to the brochure I still have, "and to discover the hidden depths of what makes us human." Profound stuff, but I am aware of a discreet sexual agenda that may be leading to a wild orgy after it is over. Surprisingly, I do not stay around to find out.

The worst fears come when I descend on escalators to the underground tube platforms. There are no thoughts of leaping under a train or anything like that. If I have to venture into the underworld, this is as close as I can physically get.

I have already crammed an incredible number of new experiences into my trip. While I appreciated exploring my emotional constraints in those confrontational workshops and huggy therapy groups, I am now aware of suppressed physical cravings, which may go beyond the accepted norms, which are crying out for gratification.

I return to Soho and embark on my first intrepid venture into the seamy side that, I hope, will teach me all the things those new age group leaders have not. I vow to experience everything at least twice before accepting my promised destiny as a wholly holy person. That can wait.

After handing over £5 to a helpful guide who guarantees me a night of passion with a "busty blonde friend" of his, I accompany him to a dimly lit alley, where I pause, only briefly. Underneath, there is a strange sense of calm, because I know that my spirit protectors, somewhere in the background, will keep me safe.

We arrive at a door with the sign, "Attractive model. Top flat." The buzzer sounds and a click lets us in. As we wind our way up the stairs, I am taken back to that time when I nervously climbed up to the attic at kindy to meet the other fabulous woman. I am picturing this one lying back languidly on a purple and gold chaise longue with black sequined drapes inviting me seductively towards her.

Standing outside the door, I am breathing rather erratically. Nervous? A little, but I knock anyway. The door opens to a moment of dashed expectations. There are two of them, one, bleached and blousy, the other, frizzled and hawk-like. Both are smoking, which isn't a turn-on. I explain that my friend – indicating behind me - but he has gone. She is certainly not going to accept the commission I paid to her now departed 'agent' as the down payment. Fifteen quid extra sounds a lot. "Shall I?" This is answered when they burst into sniggers at my naiveté which is a definite dampener on any passion that might follow.

This isn't my first time with a lady of the night, so I have no doubts I'll get it up, but their escalating giggles trigger a "Sorry, no", sending me scurrying back down past two women, near the front door, kissing goodbye - or are they men? My ability to discern such things is not yet fully honed. In Soho, I will learn quickly.

Hold on. Reading this on the computer screen, I am reminded that, yes, I am writing a spiritual autobiography and this phase of my life belongs in a quite different tome, or two. Sorry about that. A change of emphasis and a more appropriate memory sequence is coming forward now.

What I really want is a group that will provide ongoing support in a mutually respectful environment. On widening my search, I come across a brochure for a weekend residential group based on the teachings of the American, Harvey Jackins, and his Re-evaluation Co-counselling process which encourages uninhibited emotional release.

It says that I will permanently release all childhood traumas leading to a deep connection to my true purpose and an authentic future. It sounds great, and I sign up for the one remaining place. It is to be run by John Heron, the founder and director of the Human Potential Research

Project at the University of Surrey, the first university-based centre for humanistic and transpersonal psychology and education in Europe.

There are about a dozen of us waiting expectantly when John enters, a tall, dark, academic type. He explains Harvey's ideas based on immediacy which, he says will uncover and trigger off waves of emotional release.

In this kind of peer-to-peer counselling, we alternate the role of counsellor and client, working on whatever issues we choose. John wants this to be a safe space and absolute confidentiality is stressed. The peer relationship makes a considerable contribution to a sense of trust so that we can open up to and express emotions that we would steer clear of in other circumstances.

We all have distressed and repetitive forms of behaviour that are irrational, unhelpful or compulsive. Co-counselling leads to a release from these patterns, by facilitating an emotional discharge of the past experiences of hurt. Such cathartic release includes yawning, hot sweats, trembling and relaxed, non-repetitive talking.

We are told that having undivided, respectful attention often gives rise to strong feelings towards our partner. When you trust in the intimacy of a co-counselling relationship, transference is possible. Sometimes, people "fall in love". We are strongly encouraged and supported to fully experience these feelings, often leading to profound changes in how we communicate with others while developing healthier relationships in general.

Harvey realised that stuck emotions emanate from a range of different frequency levels and can be accessed and released in sequence. We sit in pairs and, when it is our turn, we notice the negatives we carry around with us and counter each of them by confidently stating the exact opposite. This brings the relevant emotions forward to be released.

Harvey's core belief is that emotions are layered through our various levels of consciousness. They can be stored up and then released sequentially through the physical body. First, yawning, which I am very good at, and coughing. This leads on to waves of hysterical laughter which arise out of embarrassment followed, usually, by torrents of tears.

I am not a natural cry baby, so this is not easy for me. They do burst out when I imagine that I am achieving what my heart desires, rather than when I am not; tears of joy, not sadness.

My first regular partner is the very attractive Malcolm. We hold hands, gradually learning trust so that we can help each other surface our hidden motives, misconceptions and recalcitrant blocks that will lead to a more spontaneous nature. It requires uncommon creative ingenuity to outwit the ego's counter-ploys.

My initial approach is to imagine myself in slightly anarchic situations that I used to do so well on stage when faced with stuffy people. I am feeling a little shy, so I assert, "I am confident." That still feels a bit held back. I repeat it, puffing out my chest and putting on a self-satisfied smile. My partner looks entirely unimpressed. I add more and more layers until I realise that acting it out doesn't work. So, I expose my actual puny chest, and suddenly I am aware of an arrogant person inside me, who really does believe that he is God's gift to humanity. I have been suppressing him all my life.

Can my partner see this? I immediately become embarrassed. "I am superior to everyone," comes next but the ridiculousness of that elicits only an awkward smile from me. Should I allow the arrogant git fully forward? I do and the escalating howls of laughter soon become tears of joy, erupting from a lifetime of feeling a total outsider.

As I delve more deeply into the mechanics of laughter, I gradually work through to the more deeply suppressed emotions beneath. Though entirely committed to life, I have always felt frustrated by it. So, I am co-counselling my authentic self to the fore and feeling the great sadness trapped beneath my still rather reserved persona.

As a child, I didn't cry, even when my mother told me that my dog, Tinker, had been knocked down by a passing car. I had to be a man, like my father, who never cried or swore or did anything remotely spontaneous.

"How dare you ignore me?" I roar at my imagined father, unable to stop waves of incredulous laughter bursting out at the thought of having actually said it – followed by a very forceful, "No one has power over me," which causes uncontrolled sobbing to take over until there is no more release left to come.

I am now in a strange altered state. A luminous blue aura appears down both sides of Malcolm's head with a face super-imposing itself on his. It looks Russian with the usual fur cap and all rugged up against the cold. I try to contact him with an excited, "Who are you, mate?" but he just smiles.

Then a voice from within tells me, "It is a past life of this man. Go to your heart and ask him to join you there." I hold this for quite a while until he dissolves into a shimmer of light.

I've read a lot about reincarnation but this is a vital step towards fully accepting its reality, an introduction to the important work I know that I'll be doing later on. But first I must make direct contact with my own past lives in order to reach beyond their limitations and discover flashes of my authentic nature, along with the source and purpose of my Earth journey.

I am now going deeper, into Harvey's fourth level of emotional release where anger dwells - not the "I hate you" kind of anger that makes things worse, but the "How dare you!" anger that releases. This anger energy doesn't attack. It is expressed widely – but, actually, there isn't much anger there in me to release. Perhaps I am already on the way to being a compassionate person, not just a passionate one.

However, there is still one more level to investigate where fear resides, and there is plenty of this to be expressed. I am jiggling and shaking now as it whooshes out. These vibrating energies seem to be coming up from deep within the earth, alternating in intensity, and demanding expression. They are clearly attached to long-suppressed memories which are now determined to escape.

Whenever I stop, the pressure very soon builds up again. If I bring anything to the fore and then hold it back, my human experience soon becomes the cruel, confrontational shadow of what it could and should be.

The more precisely I follow this routine, the more complete the release. I ask Malcolm and one of the female participants, I really like and trust,to continue meeting me regularly for the rest of my remaining time in London. With them, I share many hidden parts of my psyche while understanding that this is just the beginning of a long journey into the unknown.

※

I am still not satisfied. What about the spiritual? I return to the Quaesitor office where they tell me about a three-day 'Enlightenment Intensive' to be held at the end of my London sojourn.

Attaining enlightenment is surely why I came to England. This will be the high point of my trip, an experience that will stay with me and nourish me forever. I will return home an obviously enlightened being, and everyone will marvel. I want this more than anything but have no idea at all what it really means to be enlightened.

The following Friday evening I arrive, like an excited puppy, at the country house of one of the participants, to be met by Charlie, the monitor and cook, who takes me to a small anti-room where Jeff Love is seated, dressed in swami-like robes. He's been sent over by the Californian 'School of Ability', run by Charles Berner, who devised this western Zen process after many years of searching for the truth in the Ashrams of India.

"You take the basic question, 'Who am I?' and focus in on it precisely for the three days. You'll be woken at six in the morning when you will sit in front of a series of partners, taking it in turns to contemplate your true nature, in five-minute slots, separated by a gong. You must fully express what comes up and, at the end of fifty minutes, you change partners, repeating this for eighteen hours a day." Phew!

So it unfolds. All the mundane stuff coming first: "I am not a body", "I am a child of the universe", "I am a divine spark of creation", the usual opening gambits. There is one period in the early evening when I feel at one with everything but it soon fades. I am now aware of my insignificance in the overall scheme of things, which I counter with, "I am somebody", shouted at my partner, then "pay attention to me, you moron" comes into my mind. I hold this back. It is against the rules. No trip laying on other participants.

After the second day, mainly soul searching and painful memory, the process switches into a more abstract phase. By exploring the philosophical conflict between existence and non-existence, I am finding that the secrets of the universe are only revealed after painful perseverance beyond the point of wanting to give up. Nothing comes without staying the course and late on the second day, after battling through several wilderness periods, I reach a mini-breakthrough, "I am I." Jeff assures me that it was not an enlightenment. I need to press on beyond it.

In turn, I want my partner's hearts to open up to me. One is enough. I am not greedy - but none of them does. "Perhaps I must open up my heart to them." It is a shocking revelation, that finding my true reality is not dependent on others loving me. I must love myself first.

Early the following morning, further realisations flood in. It is clear that I only, truly, exist without thought. There is no need to analyse or explain myself. I seem to be present in every moment, allowing life to flow forward and back again. The "Who? Who? Who?" is relentless. I am determined to know my true nature but another diversion occurs. I rise up and soar Icarus-like towards the Sun. However, on surrendering to this marvellous experience, I lose faith in my ability to perform such an incredible feat, crashing to the earth with a great thud.

My past seems to be flowing out of me. My mind is oscillating between being the Lord of the Universe, the creator of everything that is, and the Lord of nothing. Then I am being drawn violently away from that into my heart and inevitable annihilation. I resist that, but not for long. Once again, I am everything and everywhere, the creator Himself and totally fulfilled.

"I am omnipotent", I proclaim loudly, "no one can destroy me." On the brink of greatness, without realizing it, I give up. I let go.

What is enlightenment? Jeff assures me that I've achieved it. I don't remember anything having happened, except a 'ping' in the background prior to the mental phenomena. I am certainly glowing and filled with light. There are no questions now. I just know, simply, that I exist, without needing anyone's acceptance to prove it. I exist entirely out of time and space, entirely in a creative state, forever achieving every facet of my true purpose even when I am not aware of it.

The rest of that final day consolidates my experience. No further doubts come up. No questions arise. I am just the everlasting, ever-present 'I', which exists far beyond the now subdued ego which I have tricked into allowing me this complete acceptance of who I truly am.

I am fully at peace with myself as I return to the 'real world'. My grotty Kings Cross hostel seems bathed in light. Over the final two days of my London adventure, I sit on tube trains, modestly accepting my fellow travellers as equals. They are staring back at me, obviously marvelling at my divine presence or, perhaps, wondering what I am high on.

This enlightened state remains with me. I have reached some kind of perfection, surely. Buddha did it. However, the inner voices tell me that I have still to learn about karma and the difficulties faced when extending this perfection out to an unresponsive world.

"What do you know? Bloody spoilsports," I snap back, before slipping back into my newfound state of bliss.

There are no direct flights to Australia and their strict quarantine regulations decree that if the plane stops even for an hour to refuel in a dodgy third world country, such as India, then I'll have to spend two weeks in a quarantine station in Australia before returning to my job. I can avoid this by staying two weeks in a 'safe' country such as New Zealand.

This isn't acceptable, of course. I have to get straight back to work. So, my cousin, Lynton. and I hatch a plan where I will travel to Auckland, arriving early in the morning, with a flight to Australia booked, later the same day, on another carrier. Hopefully, the morning staff will have gone off duty by the time I return to the airport.

I am reliving the walk towards the plane with the Zen-induced glow still obvious. I must still myself and become invisible. It is proceeding well, even though I am shaking a lot of fear out of my system as I make my way up the stairs to the cabin and my allotted seat, where I breathe a deep sigh of relief. Then, unexpectedly, I sink into a state of deep dismay. My enlightened state is beginning to retreat.

3
Home is where the Heart should be

I return to teaching the following week but I've already accepted that I can not stay in parochial Adelaide and fulfil my destiny. The enlightened me, that I enjoyed for such a short time, is still there in the background demanding that I give up my job and risk everything.

I say goodbye to my students at the end of the year. A few seem to care greatly. I have taught the co-counselling practices to my friends and begun to release most of the emotional ties to my family and my resistances to change. I'd originally intended to return to England in May but I am taking longer than expected to leap the biggest hurdle of all, telling my father that I love him. So many times, when we are playing scrabble, I open my mouth but the words just don't come out.

Months go by. Colder weather sets in. It will soon be Summer in London, which I don't want to miss, but I still have to open my heart up to my father. More co-counselling brings the realisation: I have to mean it. Is love for him really there in my heart? I'm not sure. I must dig deeper.

At the next scrabble session, unfamiliar feelings are rising up and racing around my body. Panic takes over. I look around for an escape route but when I look straight at him, "I love you!" explodes out.

He mumbles, "I love you, too", without lifting his eyes from the board.

That done, I book a one-way ticket to London in late August.

The cottage is sold and, on the evening before moving out, I am sitting in my garden sanctuary bidding goodbye to my past. All Summer, I'd slept outside regularly and developed a profound sense of connection to the inner earth, even though my old bearded protector, who lives down there, made no further appearance. Somehow, I know I'm not ready for this relationship.

My lizard friends emerge from the wall for the first time in broad daylight and venture right up to me. I extend my hand out to them and one licks it like a dog would. My heart leaps and my tear ducts are completely out of control.

There is no sadness though when my parents say goodbye to me at the airport. No feelings at all as I hold my mother while she sobs. I am entirely clear and resolute. This is a real goodbye and she knows I'm glad to be going.

❧

I am met at Heathrow airport by the delightful co-counselling couple from my first spell in blighty who had offered to put me up for two weeks in their secluded commuter belt cottage just North of London, while I get my bearings.

On the following weekend, they take me to a workshop where I meet Peter, an affable geeky guy, who is also a homoeopath and modern-day Druid, both areas that interest me. He is setting up a counselling community in his Streatham house, several miles south of the Thames river. There are three rooms left to fill before it will become a reality

On hearing this, I blurt out loudly, "One of those is mine", as I reach into my pocket to pluck out a wad of notes for my down payment. This is pushed aside.

"What the hell", I exclaim, followed by "Can't you see

how important this is?" and then "You twerp," which I don't say because Peter is already rather taken aback by my antipodean daring. He faces away and eventually responds with, "I need to think about it before making such an important decision."

I move around to where he has turned his head and look him straight in the eyes while saying the co-counselling ego-busting ploy, "Would you like to repeat that loudly?" We chortle away, sharing waves of togetherness. It is easy to break through the English reserve when you catch them off guard.

I move in a week later to join Jane and her three-year-old son, Rufus. Kate and Mel come in shortly after. It is the perfect launch for my English adventure and proves to be a very exciting and productive time for us all.

Surrounded by so many willing partners, I become a co-counselling junkie. We sometimes hold group sessions in our downstairs room. However, it is the enlightenment intensive format that attracts me the most and, early the following year, another is scheduled with Jeff Love again 'The Master'.

I am the first to arrive at a large furniture-free apartment in Grosvenor Square, overlooking the American Embassy, on the evening before it begins. Jeff speaks to me personally at length and gives me the question, 'What am I?', to contemplate.

He reminds me that enlightenment can be defined as a direct experience of our divine essence in one timeless, spaceless instant. I had already realised that the moment we are aware of it having happened, it is already out of date. There is a time lag between what our minds are aware of and what actually is, even though this is tiny.

Our essential nature exists apart from all the indirect methods that we depend on for knowing; sensing, thinking, believing, deciding, reasoning and feeling. Enlightenment cannot be consciously experienced. It lies beyond doubt and transforms our perception without words, symbols or any conceptualising.

While our spiritual seeking requires us to be two people, in a sense, there must be no awareness of separation. Someone may announce that they are "unconditional love!", but who is perceiving it? It is easy to mistake various phenomena and states of ecstasy for enlightenment, including profound stillness. They are, at best, a reaction to enlightenment, an attempt to draw it into human terms and interpret it. I am only just forming these ideas at this time, so I say nothing of this to Jeff. I am perfectly willing to go along with his process. It worked for me that previous time.

There are twelve of us altogether, equally divided. As before, we are woken at 6 am, and I sit in front of my first partner with "What am I?" already charging around in my head. I am focusing into the process with great precision and determination. This time, I want a complete enlightenment, one that lasts.

My Buddhist friends in Adelaide did not believe that my experience last time was really enlightenment at all. Scoffing, "Why, you cannot even sit in the lotus position." I agreed with them that a more lasting surrender to the divine is still ahead of me.

Jeff assures me that this is the same enlightenment that Buddha had but he had no karma left in that life to lure him away from his true nature afterwards. So, he sustained a closeness to the still, enlightened presence that is attributed to him, in every moment of his life.

This time, I know that I must go directly down into my deeper self, without any deviation. So, 'What am I'?

First comes, "I am all there is." Doubts come in immediately and I express these to my partner. It changes then to a confident, "I am all I am." Pretty obvious but this kind of certainly always fades when I try to understand it.

Jeff says that there are seven stages leading up to enlightenment that everyone goes through in some form. Stage 1 is about finding answers, mostly what we have learned from parents, teachers, ministers of religion, and friends. I presented plenty of that to a series of partners that day. Better out than in.

An intellectual approach to the question follows: stage 2 when, hour after tedious hour, I try to think things out logically and reasonably. If this is untrue, then that must be true, and so on. I know there is no "correct" answer, only the essential truth that lies behind human thought. I focus more precisely on the "what" of my existence. Every answer, valid or otherwise, is only a step towards my goal.

Then, I see how all my religious upbringing was a sham. I won the divinity prize at school, one year, by regurgitating all the religious dogma and ritual taught to me. Even then, I knew that I exist far beyond their narrow beliefs. The unlimited was always my goal.

I press on until there are no more answers. Then, I try to experience it directly, which leads on to stage 3: the phenomena. Strange visions and hallucinations spring up, spiralling energies, monsters in the corner and there is a black hole waiting to suck me in.

The intensity of the search is doing my head in. I keep drifting off, and the chap in front of me is moving in and out of focus. I can see an aura around him and a white light is streaming down to his crown chakra. Then the room appears to come alive, with walls that are undulating and seething.

"Enough of this," I cry out, as waves of emotion sweep through my body, alternating ecstasy and gloom. The gong sounds and I have to listen to another 5 minutes of my partner likewise speaking guff.

Enter stage 4: the void. I have cleared out enough of my past and have nothing more to offer by way of explanations for my existence. No thoughts are coming up. Boredom is setting in. I know I must deepen my experiences, so I look further inside which is stage 5: when I still my mind and really, really do want to experience my true nature.

I shudder suddenly and seem to be going down a level like in a lift. Every emotion and sensation is profoundly felt now. with bursts of deep sadness but no anger. There is, very occasionally, serenity. What I previously believed my human self to be is on a mission to regain lost territory, triggering off a great deal of fear and other negativity.

I am very afraid that I might realise how worthless I am, with failure all I can look forward to. My childhood terrors resurface briefly and are gone. Then the fear of death takes over. It is moving on so quickly. No chance to wallow in any of these negative ego states. I am not detached. It feels horribly real.

The relentless intention put into "What am I? becomes a jackhammer in my head. Must I be willing to die, to know what I really am? It's an easy enough question, unlike the Zen koans they use in the orient. Attempting to answer "What is the sound of one hand clapping" is a crash course in frustration. I know, I tried it once.

We are in the third day now and two of the group have already been enlightened. I remind myself that the absolute only comes when the ego gives up trying to achieve it. That is obviously not happening. I drive my determination goalwards, countering every doubt with a more subtle reasoning. The eternal void is waiting to take over.

Stage 6: I am entering into a space where the extremes are fighting for supremacy. The two irreconcilable absolutes, all or nothing, are rapidly and forcefully alternating on a quest to avoid becoming one. Then I am everything, all that is. I am reaching to the ends of the universe and, simultaneously, I am a precise point within myself where I do not exist at all, in this or any reality.

By the final afternoon, eight of the twelve had been enlightened and time is running out for me. Suddenly, my relentless activity implodes. I have turned my consciousness around, letting go of any wish to achieve or control anything. I am crying and laughing, both at once.

All thought seems to have stopped but not quite. Last time, at this point in the process, enlightenment was imminent and, soon after, I disappeared into a timeless instant, sucked to the depths of my being with a tremendous release of energy. My ego had been looking the other way and I slipped through a breakthrough moment into a state of ecstasy.

  Not this time, however. I battle on, but nothing shifts. Perhaps expectation has got in the way. The finishing bell rings soon after. Eleven out of twelve is the final tally. I am the only unenlightened one in the room.

  This unhappy chappie stays over that night with one of the illumined brigade who tells me with dancing eyes that she is an angel. I am nothing at all and have still to fully accept that wanting results is the final resistance to be surrendered.

  I keep asking myself the question, still deeply annoyed at my resolute lack of enlightenment. "What - am - I?". No answer. "I – pause – I – pause - I" before reverting back to "Who am I? This is not a step forward and I slip effortlessly into the blissy sort of state that had satisfied me the previous year but no longer can. There is more to surrender and, if bloody Buddha could get it, then so can I. "What I am" continues to taunt me with its absence.

  I dutifully spend an hour with my companion as she presents herself to me. "She can't be an angel", I had initially thought, but my disbelief melts when I see the purity shining out from her eyes. Clearly, whatever she had gone through, this is her interpretation of it, and who am I to disagree. She remains entirely within her stillness and this overwhelms all lingering reservations. The moment I stop judging, I see energy patterns extending out from her that certainly look like wings. She is an angel. No doubt about it.

  Am I jealous? Not in the least. This is not a competition. I helped her and the other ten to achieve their release. I have already surrendered to enlightenment once before. It would be greedy not to celebrate hers, so I am. We giggle a lot till I go to bed, much less angry at myself for having failed. My weary head crashes on the pillow. I insert one last "What am I?", without even a flicker in response, before falling immediately to sleep.

The next morning, dissatisfaction has returned and I grumpily come downstairs for breakfast. A few steps from the bottom, I spit out, 'What am I?', and then, "Who fucking cares?" There is my trademark 'ping' as I enter the void. A volcano erupts inside me showering energy everywhere. I am exploding and imploding simultaneously. On stepping forward, I tumble down the remaining couple of steps onto the floor, for a soft landing and no damage. I am in a lake of shimmering blue energy and sucking every last bit of it into me.

"I am love" pulsates inside. Multi-coloured energies swirl and swoop in my head and then spiral down to my heart. My whole body seems to be spinning in both directions, expanding and contracting like a concertina but with the contracting much slower than the energies revolving around. I sit laughing ecstatically. Then, and this was what really matters, the energy shoots down into the ground via the base of my spine. "I am love! Love! Love! All of me."

My ecstasy is soon intercepted by gremlins and hobgoblins, nasty little creatures, who tell me that I cannot possibly be love. Only God is love. I am...(a big wide-eyed pause)... LOVE! No doubt, no exceptions. I am nothing and everything merged. Another burst of elation follows, and then the stabilisation comes. There is nothing more to know, nothing else to be done. Love is being. Love is all.

I open my eyes to see my friend looking down intently, her face covered in an enormous smile of confirmation. As an angel, she is obviously love, too, and understands me perfectly.

I present myself fully to her for only half an hour because she has to catch a train up North. I am grounding all of the work on myself that I did in Australia. It was the down impulse balancing the up that I needed to complete. I am entirely an earth creature now. A mortal immortal - no more, no less. A symphony of the purest sound plays deep within me, and then I am sucked through a plughole into a succession of inner universes all rooted in the present moment, yet far away. In the distance, I hear, "I am love, fully and forever."

Without the mind being involved, I can focus love deep into my heart while, at the same time, releasing it gradually, smoothly, comprehensively to the waiting world. The duality of love, certainly includes the all-embracing motherly kind of love that I have rarely allowed myself to receive outside of the womb, never from the women I dated, but there is also a column of love there within me, resolutely linking the Sun to the centre of the Earth, the true 'I'.

"There is nothing but love", I confidently assert. "I am the creator of all the love there is." Love threads its way through all life, if we let it, invoking colours in a vast variety of shades. In my profoundly still and tender heart, I am aware of the soft tones of love while, at the same time, there are creative impulses coming through that will not be denied."

The firm unyielding, uncompromising nature of love's timeless expression is available to me now that I have dared to open up to it. My masculine body is filled with the gentlest love that would repel any attempt to dissipate its power, no matter what challenges I am faced with. I am both male and female but on different levels. That is the giantest revelation of them all.

I am now negotiating this diverse and complex human dimension as if in a kayak effortlessly negotiating the treacherous rapids as it slips downstream. This is the way I need to live my life.

I have missed many chances over the years to cast off my child-like self-absorption and link up with my true parents, the divine couple living deep within me, who are directing my evolution forward. They have come together today in a space shattering union. I am aware of being both entirely detached and yet, delicately positioned between those two states of ultimate being, unable to influence either, but somehow being a bridge.

Then there is one last great rush of activity and elation before the free-whirling streams stop moving as suddenly as they began. With that, comes the realisation that I am absolutely alone yet, at the same time, making millions, trillions, gazillians of connections to everything else.

Love, of course, is not an emotion. It comes from the inner stillness and is awesome in its vast possibilities. Naturally, I must allow all others their freedom to equally be love. I don't have a monopoly.

My first enlightenment transformed my life, but this one is in a different league altogether. It will remain wedded to me for the rest of my life, even during those times when I forget and doubts slip in when confronted by the many illusory things that life will throw up, demanding attention. I am beyond them, No doubt about that, yet still very human.

There is nothing more to do. I am at one with myself and I am glowing. The Zen folk refer to this steady state as "the Zen stink", lasting for weeks, as I continue to present my truth convincingly to many others. There is no desire to think. I have met up with my true nature and returned to tell the tale.

I float back home to Streatham where my enthusiasm overwhelms me as I begin to tell the rest of them what had happened. Then I get an inkling that there is still one challenge to face before the final piece of the puzzle can come forward to secure everything in place.

Enlightenment is a single non-dualistic moment and contains everything that is and could ever be. So, it is essential not to look back, or forward. 'What is' mustn't be questioned. I am sitting in a very peaceful state in the garden, the following morning when I ask myself, "What now?" The immediate response is, "Don't ask". I have committed a crucial error and doubts are flooding back in. As suddenly as love came to me, the pendulum has swung to the far ends of the universe taking love with it. I am empty, with no obvious way to regain what, it seems, I have lost.

Several desolate days go by and, still, love doesn't return. I keep away from my friends in the house. I don't want them to know that I am a fraud. I have come thousands of miles, crossed continents for this and now it has gone. It is obviously a cosmic joke, with a very unamusing punchline. I might as well go back to Australia.

After much soul-searching, I realise that in trying to make sense of my enlightenment, I have slipped back into my head. It is easy to rectify. I breathe slowly and deeply, switching attention back to my heart and, in an instant, I am absolute love again. This is the only lesson I need to learn now. Slow down, go deep into the heart and allow life to flow. It is the first of the four great simplifications to be embraced as key ingredients of my emerging spiritual philosophy.

Life in the Streatham house is working out according to plan. I spend a lot of time with Rufus, honing my fathering skills. His real dad, also part of the co-counselling network, calls round once a week, but I am Rufus's main influence. Modestly, I can say that I am a very good father. It was written on my palm that I would eventually marry and have a son. This is a trial run. Working mainly from the heart, I am developing very good nurturing skills, using the counselling ploys to draw out his deep-seated frustrations.

When Rufus grizzles, I immediately take him in my arms from behind and hold him a bit tighter than he is comfortable with. Immediately, up comes a series of emotional surges that seem to overwhelm him, and his full-hearted sobbing goes on and on until, suddenly, it stops. Then he looks around at me with sparkling eyes.

Whenever he feels more inner stuff coming up, he runs over and demands to be held. Jane and I delight in going through this emotional cleansing process in large stores. Before long, we are surrounded by a ring of angry people telling us how cruel we are and demanding that we stop him crying. What fun.

Eventually, the group rage around us is almost as

deafening as Rufus's screeching. We are terrible parents in their eyes. It becomes increasingly clear why so many people have difficulty expressing their emotions in this country. I watch other parents. Whenever their child starts to whine, in goes the dummy with the message, "I can't stand all this emotion. It reminds me of my own unresolved stuff. So, shut up, kid.".

I remember my own childhood, and the relentless attempts by my parents to keep me from being angry or crying, even when people left or died. "Goodbye is how it is," I thought, "No point in being sad." That is why I am such a no-hoper in the crying department in such situations.

I do, however, cry profusely when people come together and get the love they seek. I blubbered away at all those happy endings in the Hollywood tearjerkers, I used to see at the local Odeon. Tears of happiness were the only ones I allowed out, for others' good fortune. I still do not know how to shed a tear for unhappy endings.

Moving on to the last of Harvey's emotional releases, fear. Laugher, my easiest emotion, only releases the surface energies of embarrassment. I will get through the blocks more quickly when a much deeper fear is invoked that gets to the core of each issue. Waves of existential fear come just before a breakthrough experience - the fear of being annihilated, of disappearing forever, should death turn out to be, as the atheists contend, truly the end.

My greatest fear always comes when I try to initiate a close relationship. I believe that no one will ever want me, that my advances will be rejected by everyone who matters, till the end of time. After the first enlightenment, I still feared that the love I know myself to be will always go unnoticed but, I have become more positive during this return to England surrounded by people who care for me.

I've settled into a nice routine and I started to write the first of my plays, a West End farce that I fully expect will be snapped up for a pre-London tour by one of the many small producers who work in that field. Dream on, Greg.

My relentless nature helps me get things done. I initiate things, without having any idea of the consequences, as I explore beyond my enlightenment experiences further into the unknown. It is a roller coaster ride that I must accept.

I am totally responsible for everything that happens, I know this now. Life only offers me what I need and, deep inside, I am anticipating that my comfortable existence is about to be upended by many challenges that are designed to mature my life dramatically.

I know now that love never takes sides, never judges, never demands an outcome. It is unconditional and is, most crucially, centred in the heart – but will the support I need always be there when I expand my awareness into new areas to be opened up? Of course it will.

I don't feel that I need to reach another level of personal enlightenment, detached from my daily life. "I am love," true, but what about "We are love?" Perhaps that was what Buddha achieved, the only enlightenment that lasts.

4

Love is all there is

After six months, my involvement in co-counselling is waning. It lacks the all-important spiritual dimension. I ask my inner mentors to tell me what else I should do. When no response comes, I call out to my guardian spirits and, to my surprise, one steps forward – not fully physical, but almost. After introducing himself as Johosephat, he is reluctant to go any further.

"Don't rely on me to give you answers. Give me your answers. Use your intuition. You know everything."

"Thanks for that, matey!" I retaliate, "I thought we were friends."

All I get back is, "Just get on with it."

"Get on with what?" dogs my thoughts for days until the answer is there. "It is time to start developing as a medium." I didn't expect this, having forgotten about my previous excursion into this field.

Returning to the Spiritualist Association in Belgrave Square, there are no spirits leaping forward this time to greet me. Practical decisions are needed and I am drawn to start my psychic development with the experienced trance medium, Ivy Northage.

Before enrolling, I book a session with her spirit guide, Chan, to discuss many things that had been puzzling me since arriving in England. Above all, I want him to respond to the question, "Am I meant to be developing trance?"

"Yes", Chan confirms, "but not in the way that I am working with this medium." He explains that Ivy's mind is taken from its normal position attached to the brain and relocated just outside the body within the auric field, where it can be protected. There, she is completely oblivious to what is happening. Chan then enters on the left side and takes over the brain.

I must be detached when doing heart-inspired speaking, but an aspect of my inner mind needs to be awarely directing the process. So, deep trance mediumship is not for me. What, then, is my main expertise to be?

"Healing", says Chan, "in the widest sense of the word." He explains that I will merge my intention with the psychic energy as it comes up from the solar plexus to the heart, then on up to the shoulders and down through my hands.

I accept this, but Ivy isn't a healer and doesn't teach this. Should I stay with her? Chan advises me, "Yes, you do need to understand all the psychic gifts so that you will be able to work with those who have them. You will develop the clairsentient energy that lies in the solar plexus region so that you will use gut feelings as an adjunct to your healing ability. You will know exactly what to do. Also, you can develop a precise contact with your healer guide when in her circle." I agree to stay.

When I start something, I soon develop an almost compulsive commitment to it. Ivy runs her circle with Wynn Kent, a very masculine colour therapist who balances her. I am receiving a very thorough basic training with them.

Trance remains my greatest interest. I go to every one of Chan's monthly lectures and regularly attend his personal development sessions where he teaches me a great deal about how the spirit realm operates and how communication between the worlds is engineered.

I attend many other groups and events, to gain a full spiritual understanding, which includes a visit to Alexandra Palace, where the 15-year-old guru, Maharaj Ji, and his Divine Light Mission family give me the "Knowledge." I quickly realise that such Eastern practices are of no interest to me. Even, Krishnamurti does not impress when he explains to me, in person, why he needed to break away from the Theosophists. There seems to be a lot he is still trying to avoid.

Though Janov's Primal Scream is much more interesting and relevant, I doubt that the young London group leader has had much formal training. So, can he be trusted? On the phone, he assures me that he has been to America and participated in one of Janov's workshops. I agree to meet him in a semi-derelict East London building.

On the way there, I ask for directions from a respectable-looking chap who turns out to be John Profumo, the notorious lover of Christine Keeler. After resigning as a politician he became the chief fundraiser for the nearby Toynbee Hall, which helped to restore his reputation.

I tell him about what I am about to embark on and he listens without commenting. Then a young woman passes by, and he turns his head briefly.

"It is so difficult to control one's natural urges when an attractive woman comes along." He looks down and smiles wistfully with, I suspect, a tear lurking in the background. I am surprised at how ordinary and reserved he seems. Not a great lover type at all. He wishes me luck.

The young man is very pleased that I have responded. "You are my first," he says, as takes me to a padded room. "We are all creatures of need," quoting Janov, "and when those needs are not met as children, we create neuroses, obsessions, anxieties and depression." I point out that this seems to be a method of controlled catharsis using a heightened arousal technique of the sort used by sects to brainwash and subdue believers. His answer doesn't entirely convince but he seems a nice chap.

I follow his instructions to throw myself against the padded walls as if trapped in a womb, but, when the sound comes, it is not a scream, much more like a wolf's howl as it emerges from some cavernous part of my being. It surprises and alarms the young man far more than it does me. I know that I will return to this kind of experience again but, right now, Janov is not for me. It would interfere with my psychic development.

It is strange. The more I develop psychically, the less aware I am of those beings who work with me. Ivy tells me that I will not be a clairvoyant in the usual sense. I will no longer see spirits using the third-eye chakra, except at crucial times. I accept this. Spirit is there and I don't need to see or hear them objectively.

I focus in the heart where a rich world of instinctive connection with the subtle planes is available to me and I must let this understanding manifest in my life.

I have been very happy in the Streatham community with people who care for me but our landlord, Peter, has become immersed in his Druid practices. We rib him mercilessly when he dons white robes to go to the Summer solstice celebrations at Stonehenge. His homoeopathic mentor is a leading figure in the Druid movement. I am fascinated by their ancient traditions but something inside is saying, 'No. Not yet'.

Enlightenment intensives remain my main interest. I participate in another with Jeff Love, on a yacht moored on the Thames,.Its effect on me continues to be profound and I am eager to discover more. Later, I learn that the originator of the system, Charles Berner, is coming over to run one in a disused schoolhouse near Leeds with 60 participants mainly bussed in from London.

This time, I am given "What is another" to work on, which is the obvious step to convert my Self-enlightenment into a state that synchronises with the needs of others. Then I will be (a little) more like Buddha.

I expect this to be a vital step in my spiritual development but I certainly do not warm to Berner when he takes on his enlightened master role and gives one of his talks. He positions himself above us, aloof and distant. Monitors are doing most of the work.

On the first day, we are all trying to reason out the answer. I am pitting why I do not exist against why I do, setting up a tension between the two, until this breaks. I am coming from the heart and attempting to refine my understanding using intuition rather than mental processes, but some strong activity in the base chakra area is confusing me. I am having only small realisations and it is very difficult to build up enough tension for a breakthrough.

The strength of the Jeff Love-ins was their intimacy. Trust was built up between participants because, if you are going to let go and reveal your inner self, you must feel safe. In this draughty assembly room, we are placed in front of a succession of different partners with no chance to establish an ongoing rapport with any of them.

I still don't fully understand how the process works. Berner's remoteness is making it more difficult and enlightenment remains out of reach. I am aware of only two participants who had a full breakthrough experience. I leave very disappointed.

In the Streatham house, I am still very happy surrounded by people who care for me. My relationship with Jane continues to flourish, especially when helping her to bring up her son, Rufus. I am becoming a very effective father, a role I expect to continue when I marry but, of course, this will not be to her.

There are shifts happening in the growth movement generally. A large number of therapists and group leaders have tuned to a charismatic Indian spiritual teacher, the "sex guru", Bhagwan Rajneesh, who has an ashram in Poona. Many are seeing this as a way to liberate themselves from their traditional English reserve.

Clare and Paul Lowe, the founders of Quaesitor, are always on the lookout for the next big thing. They fly off to India to check him out. Whole organisations in the growth movement are closing down because their leaders are overseas and there is no one left to run them. Clare and Paul become devotees, changing their names to Poonam and Teethra.

On their return, they set up the Kalptaru centre in Chalk Farm and Poonam convinces Jane to become involved. One evening, she returns home dressed in saffron robes. I immediately imagine myself as Guru Greg. "Oh no," she says pointedly, "He is an enlightened master and you certainly are not."

Soon after, I call a house meeting and point out that Merle has not been participating in any activities. He is doing no co-counselling with any of us and is generally an absentee housemate. We unanimously agree to give him one month's notice. He doesn't object.

An ad is placed on the notice boards in all the growth centres to find a replacement and there is just one applicant, David, who has just returned to London from art college. He is very keen to open up to his spiritual self. He moves in and, though not particularly interested in co-counselling, he is eager to do an enlightenment intensive. We engage Jeff Love to run one, in our downstairs room, that November.

No one actually gets enlightened but, near the end, something powerful rises up in me that is impossible to ignore. I am in front of David and still grappling with "What is another?" when it suddenly becomes "There is only one other." A shaft of energy shoots straight down through me and goes on and on, far into the earth. When I look into David's eyes, my heart zings. I know that my love is for him. No doubt at all.

In love with a man? This is new to me but I know that there isn't anyone else in the world I want to be with. Scary. Impossible, of course. He is heterosexual and fresh out of a relationship with one of the other students. This is a nightmare in the making - to love with this intensity and not to be able to live it.

"I am love," I shout. "We are love. Love is all," and I start laughing at the absurdity of the situation. I only cry when people come together, so the inevitable tears pour out of me uncontrollably.

I don't expect David to release his own emotions when confronted by mine but, suddenly, he comes over and holds me, "Oh baby, baby, let go of your tears, let go of your fears." He then rocks me backwards and forwards, intoning tunefully, "Let go now." His breath is slowly exhaling as he does this.

I doubt that he is aware of what he is doing, but I am experiencing something incredible. My mouth opens and the howl starts up again, coming from a far deeper place inside me, as if echoing through a rocky canyon. I am not forcing it. I'm not even aware of being involved at all. It goes on and on, coming and going in waves. Then David lets go of me and I snap out of it.

He apologises but I say, "It's fine. We were carried away. All part of the process." Then the gong rings to end the intensive. My ecstatic feelings have retreated now and David goes over to thank Jeff Love. A very deep place in both of us had been accessed and I hope we will return to it later.

Am I gay? Are these feelings real? Harvey Jackins, in his recent book, contends that it is possible for a heterosexual man, suddenly confronted by such feelings, to co-counsel himself out of them. This is one of the things I will confront him with when I attend his imminent four-day retreat in a country house near Arundel. Janov also claims to "fix everything from alcoholism and menstrual cramps, to homosexuality".

I believe that all desires come from deep unfulfilled needs which resonate with our true nature. When pounding the padded walls of that cell, and the energy rebounded at me, I did wonder what is hidden deep inside of me. It seemed to be the complete opposite of what I had previously known myself to be.

It is Harvey Jackins' turn to justify his teachings. Some 50 of us turn up at his late Summer retreat eager to learn more but, in the breaks, I notice that his English representative, John Heron, is criticising his mentor and rubbishing some of his ideas. I like Harvey, but even I am concerned that he is going too far in believing that all behavioural patterns are suspect and can be co-counselled clear.

One of my co-counselling partners is a lesbian. She

publicly asks him whether he stands by his statements on homosexuality in his book, which she reads out. He confirms unequivocally that it is an aberration and states that if his methods are followed the client will eventually return to normal. She asks him to prove it. He says that he will continue with this after the meal break, during which there is heated discussion going on in small groups.

Most of us feel that Harvey has taken his otherwise laudable beliefs too far. It is like saying that a black person could be co-counselled to being white. He eventually said that several of his gay clients had turned straight and the only way to test his beliefs is to keep going with the co-counselling release.

Even though the process is still working for me, John Heron is dissatisfied with Harvey's ideas and he is starting a breakaway group. The son rebelling against the father. In a formal letter to the community, he sets out what he sees as important differences between the two approaches and he invites all the English members to join him. I am not convinced by any of this, so I decide to retreat from the network.

Returning to Streatham, David is not there and I go to bed trying to come to terms with what has happened and apprehensive about the future. In the enlightenment intensives, I had removed all limitations on how I could open up to love and I know that what I have been feeling is real and cannot be pushed aside. If ever I needed a co-counselling session, it is now.

I have probably awakened a past life memory. I can see a young man, in a very conservative village in Northern Italy, with domineering parents. He is very unsure of himself but manages to escape to a more open life where he meets a young woman visiting from Rome. They fall in love. This was David, and Jane was my formidable and very jealous mother who did not want us to be together.

I hear the front door close, David comes into my room and sits on the side of the bed. He asks if I am O.K. There is an awkward silence and then I risk it, touching him ever so gently on the cheek. Almost immediately, he slides in beside me and my arms enfold him. Nothing is said. We lay there hardly moving, hardly breathing.

"This is new to me", he whispers, and it takes some hours before he relaxes enough and I can feel us switching into a much deeper soul connection. Love is taking over entirely.

"I don't want it to be sexual. That's not what I am feeling."

"No," I assure him, "it is something far deeper."

In the stillness, he is giving far more to me than I believed possible. Indeed, on some level, we are dancing in a cosmic ballroom with a celestial orchestra providing the soundscapes with the whirling and openness releasing my soul.

'This is true love," I tell him, "forever and ever."

We spend that night together, giggling well into the early hours, but my room is directly below Jane's. She has probably heard us and sussed things out. The next morning, as we pass Kate's door, from the few words I overhear, we are the subject of a co-counselling session.

Afterwards, Jane comes to my room and says, "I can't stand the thought of you being together. I don't want it. Stop doing it." She leaves, but the feelings are too overpowering.

When I hear her shouting from upstairs, I think of the past Italian life where she refused to let me be with the one I loved. "I know it is a challenge for her," I shrug, "but, she has to learn." I am yet to understand that while it is fine to challenge someone, if asked to stop, you must. We are being very cruel.

Then there is a scream from upstairs followed by the smashing of glass. Jane has slammed her fists against the glass pane in her door. We race upstairs. Blood is pouring from her arms. I panic, overwhelmed by shame.

Peter takes her to hospital, leaving David and I with much to decide. One thing is certain, he still wants to be with me. When Peter returns, he tells us that they are keeping Jane in for observation but she will be all right.

We breathe a sigh of relief until he says that he is giving us until the end of the week to leave the house.

It is almost Christmas. Where in the hell can we go? I think of a woman on the Enlightenment course who lives with her husband in a three-story house in a posh western suburb with an empty basement. A phone call confirms that they will put us up for six weeks. After that, they will be converting it into a flat to let it out.

ઝ

1975

From there, we decide that squatting is our best option. There are many empty commercial properties around needing renovation and the owners probably feel it is better to have someone in there than leave them empty.

We visit the squatters group off Balls Pond Road who inform us of our rights and how to avoid being arrested or evicted, once inside. They also give us a list of vacant properties. We want to be right in the centre of things, so a house in Warren Street, number 38, is the obvious choice.

The following Sunday night we arrive with hammer and jemmy, ready to break in. David is the courageous one and leads the way over the back fence on Euston Road. The basement rooms are screened off by metal bars, so we climb up the drainpipe to the ground floor and look in, yes, absolutely deserted. We easily prise a window open.

It has been an incredibly smooth operation. The next morning, David buys a lock and we fix a notice to the front door proclaiming our legal right to be there.

So, what have we acquired? On the ground floor, there is a large, once ornate space that was probably a sitting room before it went commercial. In the front office, there is a well-crafted desk and swivel chair on a grubby old grey carpet and even a battered old typewriter that I can write my plays on.

Upstairs, there is a fully functioning kitchen, plus two cheaply-panelled rooms and a loo. The water is connected, thankfully, but there is no bathroom. To shower, we sneak into the University College in Gower Street with student facilities and a gym in the basement. No one twigs this and we adjust easily to this clandestine lifestyle.

It was an incredibly exciting time. Carnaby Street is only a shell of its former self but in many rooms and basements around Soho and in squats nearby, the creative life is buzzing. I embrace this unconventional lifestyle unreservedly.

David has a few months before finishing his post-graduate art studies at the Slade, so he takes a part-time driving job to pay for his clay and kiln hire. I help him set up a sculpting studio in the large downstairs room and he is teaching me the basics of his craft. To my surprise, I am a natural. I fashion a very lifelike bust of him and he responds with an even more realistic one of me.

David lacks confidence in his own ability and I have to regularly tell him how good his sculptures are – which they are. I sense that his creativity had been stifled in many female lives. Back then, women weren't supposed to be good at anything except needlework and looking after babies. This life in a male body is meant to balance the female sensitivity in him with a more confident masculine creative nature - but the frustrations from the past remain. Not sure of his place, he becomes very angry at times. I often expect him to lash out.

Despite this, things proceed very smoothly. He isn't at all interested in the psychic world, so I accompany him to exhibitions, openings, arty parties and bohemian pubs. Soho is only a ten-minute walk away and it becomes our mutual stamping ground.

I have regular sittings with Chan but when I try to discuss reincarnation, he cannot get what I need through Ivy because her approach to the subject is entirely different from mine. Although she can't consciously interfere, the belief patterns in her brain are getting in the way. He does confirm my special gift for delving into the past and negotiating its complexities. Indeed, discerning past karma in others has already become my fascination.

It must have taken a lot of lives together to build up the strength of love that is now taking David beyond his natural heterosexual nature. I doubt that he will have any more relationships of this kind in the future but, right now, it is everything I could possibly hope for.

"How long will we be together?", I ask Chan. "Four years, when he will meet a woman to love and you will start preparing to meet your future wife, also."

Living on the margins of respectable society, I am reminded that many in the human family are still engaged in the project to pretend that we are independent beings separate from each other and our surroundings. I am using David to delve into the mysteries, without him realising it.

I follow up on my interest in past lives. This time, on slowing down and extending the out-breath, I experience an incredible pull down from my base chakra deep into the earth. I am shaking a little. There is a presence there that needs releasing. Something evil, is it? It doesn't feel so.

I am fully rooted in the earth. Then, a cavernous sound seems to be coming from the solar plexus, right up into my throat. More shaking. It's the fear again. Despite this, I am learning to balance in the heart, reaching up and down equally from there along a central column of consciousness, That's it. Balance is the key.

That night, while lying close to David as he sleeps, Johosephat reappears.

"I am one of your guardians," he informs me, "and I have been appointed to take you through your training. I will bring forward each of the past lives that you and David have had together, one by one. Eight in all. Then you will see how the love you have for each other has developed over time.

I already have an innate understanding of how reincarnation works. I have never subscribed to the idea that there is a single soul moving from one incarnation into another. I see them as semi-independent beings linked to a source self, rather like the tentacles of an octopus with the present life being the only one that reaches down to earth.

"So, they will be coming forward individually to talk to me. Are you the only guardian there with me in this project?"

"No, there is always a team of us involved, but I have the most experience in working close to the earth. Others will come later when you are ready to begin to serve humanity with us."

That night, the first of a series of doors to the past opens and I focus in on what lies beyond. A scene builds up between us. I am a young Egyptian man with little understanding of the world. I like to sit on the banks of the Nile, hoping that its power will come into me one day. Through the reeds, I see this young lass, kneeling, and washing her hair. It is love at first sight. No doubt at all, but I am too shy to approach.

I go to the same spot regularly, hoping to see her again and, some weeks later, she appears from out of the reads, spinning around, joyously free. My heart spins with her. I pluck up the courage to speak to her and discover that she is an illegitimate daughter of the Pharaoh who likes to slip away from her minders whenever she can. Unfortunately, I am a mere village boy and so, a serious relationship is impossible.

We meet there whenever she can but, after several months, she stops coming. My heart shrinks with the loss. I ask around and learn that she sometimes passes by when coming from the palace in a formal procession. I am always there to cheer her on, but she doesn't see me.

The next time, I venture out onto the road enough to be fully visible. She waves to me and smiles. I stay there transfixed until I am dragged back into the crowd by some guards and knocked to the ground. It was worth it though. The connection has been made in our hearts and, although we never speak again, I continue to live my life for her and do not marry.

I want to talk to David about this, but I know he will not believe and, worse still, knowing that I am watching him, he may want to sleep in another room.

A few nights later, another of his female lives is there. We are sisters and high-class courtesans in 8th century Greece. I have seen her before. It doesn't appeal to me that I might ever have incarnated as a woman. What a strange idea. I am sure it didn't happen very often.

In this life together, we attract wealthy and influential men, encouraging them to be open and generous when relating to us. My political sensibility and acumen is much more effectively honed in this life than when I am actually in a political position.

Next, we are both young monks in 9th-century Tibet. He is a very sensitive soul and regularly comes to me for support. I act like his big brother even though he is a year older. However, arrogance gets the better of me and I attempt an advanced spiritual practice before I am ready. It goes out of control, affects my brain, and I pass over at the age of 28. He is devastated.

Two more male/female lives followed: in Russia where we are both revolutionaries and in China where we go to the other extreme and put down dissidents. This is interesting, these reverse experiences, being a perpetrator and a victim in different lives, but this is necessary if we are to have a completely lived understanding.

Then on to a very significant life in France, when we are again both female. I am the wife of a rich aristocrat. David is my maid and close companion. More precisely, I am a lesbian and this is a marriage of convenience.

I live in a separate wing of the very large house and make little contact with the stream of my husband's dissolute friends who visit him at all hours for their noisy bouts of debauchery. I manage the household very efficiently, but things are not going so smoothly outside. There are many demonstrations against the ruling class and the gossip, at Parisian women's soirees, indicates that it is much more serious than my husband and his male associates are aware of.

I decide it is a good time to visit some wealthy friends in England, taking my maid with me along with some jewels and two valuable heirlooms belonging to my husband. I set up house and continue to live a high life. I pass my maid off as an impoverished cousin. Soon after, word comes of the first violent outburst in Paris. We do not return and I learn that my husband has gone to the guillotine.

I join a group of what would now be called feminist women playwrights, who give a different slant on the drawing-room comedies, the machinations of love and lust, with the men as figures of ridicule. However, the money fetched in selling the jewels is running out. Fear of destitution arouses a great deal of insecurity which I compensate for by over-eating, Indeed, I put on a lot of weight which may be why, in this life, I like to keep as slim as possible.

It is now a few years later when a horse drawing a milk cart goes out of control and careers towards me. I am not fast enough to get my bulky body out of the way. A pain shoots through me as I am knocked down and crushed to death - at the early age of, again, 28. No happy ending there, either.

Lying beside David, I am gradually sensing the patterns and structure of what motivates us from behind the scenes. I can see how all of these former lives work together. There is a destiny plan woven into our subtle bodies which sends out an ongoing invitation for life to respond to our needs. We create our opportunities from the inner planes and then must meet them halfway in life.

So, this relationship of ours was meant to happen, though not certain to happen. There is always free will. We could have backed away and the opportunity would have passed us by unrecognised – but, fortunately, this union was well prepared for on other levels, and the decision to explore a magical life together was virtually inevitable. For the first time in my life, I am entirely content.

5

I meet my guides

It is late August when David opens a letter and lets out an explosive "Yes. Yes. Yes!!!", punching the air repeatedly. He has been accepted into a postgraduate course at the Falmouth Art College.

"Where is that?" is my casual response, expecting it to be close to London.

"Right at the tip of Cornwall", he informs me. "Six hours away by train. I will be starting in just over two weeks' time."

After a long 'taking it in' pause, I respond, "Wonderful news." It is a lie, of course. I am shattered but mustn't show it. I can see how happy he is. We've had ten marvellous months together, and it isn't the end, he assures me. Next July, he will have his certificate and we will get back together again as if nothing has happened.

I wave a tearless goodbye to him on Paddington Station until my hand almost drops off and I return to the large semi-derelict house that I no longer want to call home. The front door slams shut with the sound echoing throughout as it always has but this time I am aching and alone.

൞

It is my aim to set up a healing and psychic centre and, as a start, I offer to help Ivy build up her teaching school. She says that this is not necessary. It is clear that she wants to keep complete control over her operation. Perhaps it is time to look for someone more compatible with my aims.

I lose no time in arranging a sitting with Chan and, after giving me a heart-to-heart about my psychic progress, he agrees that I have gone about as far as I can in Ivy's circle. My guides want me to leave when the term ends. There is another opportunity coming, he assures me, with a medium more appropriate for my development.

"A trance medium?", I probe.

"Oh, most definitely, but with some rather special abilities."

˜

1976

Cut adrift by Ivy, I continue my search for her replacement. I contact the editor of the Psychic News hoping to hear about someone who can channel my own guides and also my dead relatives. He assures me that there is no one who can do that any more, which is confirmed by the head of the Spiritualists National Union. I am stymied.

Fortunately, these 'experts' haven't a clue. While eating a freshly prepared meal in the Spiritualist Association basement café, a member of Ivy's circle comes over to sit with me. We talk about the difficulties both of us are having with our development. She needs a session with Chan to discuss this but Ivy is booked up many months ahead. Fortunately, I have arranged one that I no longer need. I offer it to her.

I explain that I am looking to replace Ivy with someone with a wider range of gifts. I outline my wish list and vent my frustration at not being able to find anyone suitable.

"Oh, I know someone like that", she assures me. "Maisie Besant is easily the most versatile medium around. She does trance, healing, transfiguration, psychic surgery and there's another." She thinks for a while, "Like exorcism, but different, not religious. Yes, she calls it rescue work."

This sounds promising. "Then she knows about reincarnation."

"An expert. Again, she calls it something else. I don't remember what that is."

I take her hand gratefully and say thanks to all of the spirits that I assume have engineered this meeting. I ring Maisie for a sitting and this is arranged for three months' time.

∽

David wants to do another enlightenment intensive. I ask around and there is one being held this coming Easter. He arrives in London ahead of this. There is an internship available at the Royal Academy, and he is one of two finalists. Eventually, it goes to the nephew of the Chair of the Governing Council. Isn't that always the way?

David makes friends with the Goths who live in the squat next door and they invite us to drop in for an evening meal. I had often seen them go out late, dressed in their black, I shouldn't say costumes, because they seem very serious, with their pale faces and lots of eye shadow. They are getting ready when we arrive. I realised then that on the surface I am a rather conventional sort of bloke, and not cut out for their kind of flamboyant lifestyle.

The Intensive is being held in a large basement flat in East London. I am in for a shock. Poonam Lowe is in charge. My immediate impulse is to leave. I am told that she has been trained to run them in India but I believe it is important for the "Master" to be more enlightened than those attending. I rather doubt that she is but David really wants to do it. As I am something of an enlightenment junkie, I agree to participate.

My fears are justified though. Poonam has added some of Baghwan's boisterous physical meditations and she is confrontational. This is quite the opposite of Jeff Love. The bathroom doors are not lockable.

She often pops in to track people down, without knocking. It doesn't faze me at all, but is it necessary?

I go back to doing "What am I?" The alternative, "What is another" might be too difficult in this environment. I switch into neutral when participating in the Baghwan's dynamic meditation which ends up with everyone going wild. A powerful release exercise but this isn't the place for it.

Undaunted, I forge ahead in my usual fashion and, just after dinner on the second day, I am on the brink of a non-physical state when there is a very small 'Ping'. I say to my partner. "I am beyond sex." Pure energy erupts inside of me and, afterwards, I am incredibly peaceful.

I go to 'Master' Poonam to present my truth, expecting it to be validated.

Instead, she retorts, "What rubbish. You are no such thing." I am rather stunned. Flabber and gast have yet to come together and I am unable to say a word in response.

So, I repeat, "I am beyond sex." My lack of doubt unnerves her.

"You can believe what you like but I am sure you aren't."

I don't know how to continue. Thoughts race around in my head until it suddenly makes sense. She is a bioenergetics practitioner who launched encounter groups in London and she has prostrated herself at the feet of the sex guru. I shouldn't have expected anything else. Of course, I should leave right now, but David is here and I don't give up easily.

Soon after, she herds us all into a circle and orders us to take our clothes off. Then we are told to say, to the rest of the group, all the negative things we feel about them, so that we can be loving towards them for the rest of the time. Of course, this is a travesty of the Berner enlightenment process but, in my blissful state, I feel no urge to resist.

I don't actually have a negative thought in my head as I face the other participants hurling abuse at me. I open my heart to all of them. The more they shout at me, the more expansively I say, "I am love. I love you," which makes Poonam even angrier.

"Say what you really feel, Greg," she demands.

"I am beyond all of that, " I repeat, every time she taunts me.

"Get out all your shit. You must have some in there. You're human, aren't you?"

I look up for inspiration. Light, streaming in through the ceiling, highlights our nakedness and the floor becomes a chasm of contentment into which I fall.

Poonam slides a chamber pot behind me. "Go on, show me what's inside you." I smile back at her. Angry now, she sends David across with the demand, "You know what you think. Give it to him!"

I hear what David says, how frustrated he is that I am not a woman. Only then can he really love me. I don't flinch. I feel no hurt but I know that this is some kind of turning point. What kind of intimacy can I expect with him now?

I stubbornly stay till the end, hoping that I can reach an even more profound level but, of course, in those circumstances, that can't happen.

The enlightenment process is still important for me but Jeff Love has returned to America, and there is clearly no one in England with the spiritual maturity to support me through it. It may be the last Enlightenment Intensive I attend.

When David and I get back home to our squat, and he has fallen asleep, I ask for another of our lives together to come forward. I need to get the best out of what has happened so that our relationship can move forward.

I am immediately aware that we were part of an itinerant group of musicians and performers who toured the villages of Romania. I played an instrument and David, then a woman, sang beautifully. This may partly explain my interest in writing musicals in this life, but it isn't relevant to what has been happening recently.

I am then firmly told by my inspirers that there is only

one more life to come forward, but we still have work to do on ourselves before it can.

I am full of pent-up needs when I visit Maisie at her Wood Green home. I have no idea what to expect. Many mediums of this period are quite nondescript, as if a strong personality and ambition will get in the way of them being vehicles for clear spirit communication. The figure who opens the door is in her sixties and does not initially give off the vibrancy I am hoping for.

I am the forceful, no-nonsense one. "I have come to speak to one of my guides, not yours," I announce, not realising how provocative this is.

Looking into her eyes, I see the inner depths. She responds very firmly, "We'll see what I can do about yours but you will have to talk to my own guide first, Feca." She points to a framed drawing on the wall of a thin-faced chap with a bright red fez and jovial eyes. There are many other psychic portraits around the room. "That's my healer guide, Ming and this is St Luke. He helps me with the rescue work."

Maisie then sits me down opposite her and closes her eyes. "Blessings, dear friend," starts our discourse. "You want to meet one of your own guides. There are seven here today making up your main team. There's your North American Indian healer guide and your Tibetan spiritual teacher." I sense someone close to my left shoulder, but I can't make out who it is.

Maisie stops to attune deeper, "You may not be aware of your African doorkeeper who normally stands back. He protects you. And your Egyptian guide who will bring through the philosophy. There is also one who wishes to speak to you now."

"My name is Li Kwan, your brother in China during the Ming dynasty. I was the mandarin responsible for a region not too far from what is now Bejing. You were the black sheep of the family." Of course, what else would I be? He confirms that I won't be clairvoyant in the usual sense but I do need to sense spirit and relate intuitively to those who come to me from his side of the veil. He will help me with this.

Before I can thank him, he unexpectedly asks, "Do you want to know what happened to your lizards?"

"Of course I do," explodes out of me. I am shaking my head in stunned amazement.

"Well, they're over here now. The new owners pulled down the wall and they died in it. And they wish you to know that they will not leave you while you are in your earth body."

The proof I'd been waiting for, not of survival after death but that there are beings watching over me, aware of what I am up to and who care for me, not figments of my imagination. Maisie could not possibly have guessed the lizards. She is definitely the medium I've been looking for.

Maisie serves the spiritualist churches but has no reputation beyond that. Indeed, I discover later that she is seen as a bit of a troublemaker, always speaking her mind. I am already feeling just how different and impressive she is. A kindred soul.

Another appointment is made for a few weeks' time when I can grill her inspirers with the long list of questions I am already devising. But, on arriving there, Maisie is strangely reluctant to engage.

I sense that she is aware that this is a major turning point for her, after a life spent in the very limited spiritualist world with friends who are not at all interested in her unusual psychic abilities. I will introduce her to a younger, more adventurous crowd who will help her explore new ways of expressing her subtle gifts.

She eventually opens up and talks about her life as a Christian and how this is compatible with being a spiritualist. "Jesus was the greatest medium and healer who has ever walked the planet," she asserts.

Maisie's early training was with Miss Moyes at the Greater World Spiritualist Church during the war, but she had fallen out with her over reincarnation.

"She didn't believe in it at all, and I had very firm beliefs that my guides had given to me."

As reincarnation is already my main interest, I need to know whether her ideas match my own which I pour out, eager for her reaction. After a long pause, she confirms that, yes, that is her understanding, too.

"My guides call it Serial Consciousness. When needing to access detailed past life information, I visit the akashic records in my sleeping hours which I will reveal to you in a later sitting, if you would like that."

Would I like? You couldn't keep me away. "When? Next week? I can come any time." She holds her hands up indicating that patience is needed.

Akashic records? Back in the library, I learn that they are where the memories of past lives are stored. Do I access these records when I pick up information about my former existences? Possibly, but this only comes in flashes, isolated moments of knowing. I am not in touch with a celestial librarian giving me detailed information. More likely, these former lives are around me, slipping this information through when they can.

At the next sitting, Li Kwan explains the way he wants to work with me. I had thought that, with clairvoyance, you look outwards through the brow chakra into the subtle worlds but he says that the best way is to focus inwards enabling the outer information and impressions to register deeply there. Everything in spiritual seeking may seem to be paradoxical. When focussing into the heart, energy is directed out automatically on a more subtle level. "This is important to understand when loving your enemies."

"I don't have any enemies," I maintain.

"Oh," he responds mischievously, "there are a few on this side who don't like you very much."

He then makes way for my Red Indian healer guide. I am aware of a sphere with a multitude of rays of light coming out from the periphery.

He tells me that it is my task to introduce new ways of

healing to the world that focus more deeply into a health condition, getting right at the cause. I haven't begun developing as a healer, so I have nothing practical to base his advice on. He will come close in my mediation times and impress on me how to proceed. Only, I don't meditate.

He is prompting me to ask Maisie if she holds a development circle. She doesn't and adds, "I'm not sure I have the time." Fortunately, the following week, two other sitters ask the same question and the group starts several months later.

Maisie is a very ordered woman. She serves the spiritualist churches every Sunday and runs a healing clinic with her husband, Edwin, on Monday evenings. They do the rescue work on Tuesday when trapped spirits speak through her and he grapples with their issues so that they can move on. Maisie does private sittings on Wednesday afternoons followed by this Thursday development class and her reincarnation sessions on Fridays.

In the development circle, Maisie tells us how her trance works. "I'm not one of those who get taken out of it. That kind of mediumship is on the way out. It must be a collaboration now".

That idea is new to me. "So, you can hear what is happening."

"Yes, but I don't get involved. I keep my attention very still and make sure I don't interfere. That's the kind of trance you'll be doing."

It sounds easy enough until I try it in the circle. We close our eyes and, after a while, Maisie positions herself in front of one of the women, holding her hands up in support. "Welcome friend. I can see you there. Have you anything to say?" A few words are spoken, then silence. A bit later, Maisie comes over to me and repeats the same invitation. I can't even manage a mumble.

It goes on that way for six years without me saying a word. I am incredibly dedicated. Fortunately, I am having more success with the healing.

You may have noticed that I have not mentioned the stars, the main subject of this book, or my venerable old spirit companion from inside the earth. Somehow, all of this was forgotten. I asked Maisie why he had retreated. Her response was "The time still isn't right for you to work together. Have patience." For a while I did and so, dear reader, must you.

ॐ

Edwin is two years younger than Maisie and still employed, so it isn't until I arrive for my first Thursday evening development group that we meet. I get on well with most of the people I meet on a casual basis but, from the outset, he certainly isn't warming to me. I ask Maisie for her view on this.

"Oh, he prefers to talk to the girls", she casually informs me. I know there is more to it than that and I tell her so. "Karma", she adds. "There is always karma when people don't get on. You will both have to work through it."

"I was a judge, wasn't I?", comes up immediately.

"Yes, and not a good one. You shut him up in jail at the behest of some of your cronies and he died there." Copenhagen comes to my mind. "You are very perceptive. That was indeed where it was. But then, he was your father in another life when he abandoned your mother and you kids to a life of destitution."

Edwin is always courteous when I visit but our relationship remains awkward with tense undercurrents always preventing relaxed communication.

Maisie's main spirit guide was the Egyptian Pharaoh, Akhenaten. I take up the many opportunities to discuss deeper matters with him. I am particularly interested in his attempt to deal with the inequities in the authoritarian class system of his day and to reform the priesthood which flourished within it.

He tells me that Edwin, in that life, was his father, Amenhotep III. It was his structures of power that

Akhenaten was seeking to change. Maisie had been Edwin's wife then, too. The formidable Queen Tiye. In some ways, she still is. It was his illegitimate daughter that my former life had fallen in love with.

Back in London, memories flood in when I visit the British Museum to view the Egyptian artefacts from the Akhenaten times, the statues and the sarcophagi. I am also drawn to the Greek period, and especially to a small marble statuette of Socrates where "He was my teacher," comes to mind. Then, after a pause for reflection, "I am absolutely certain of it" follows

Maisie can channel just about any spirit person who is willing. "Can I speak to Socrates?", I ask. "We'll have to see," she replies and closes her eyes. The chap who comes instead introduces himself as Crito. He speaks at some length about my past life when I was Socrates' eldest student. He tells me to look at Michelangelo's painting of that time, I would see him there holding the abacus. Sure enough, he does look incredibly like me.

All the elite men of Athens were expected to have an intellectual pursuit, a sporting ability and a creative outlet. Crito gave mine as mathematics, long-distance running and sculpture. In my current life, I passed pure mathematics to second-year level at university, though I did not have the abstract mind needed to go further. I subsequently taught maths at secondary school level for 11 years which now seems a waste of my talent, even though it did help me develop confidence.

I taught mainly from the heart which meant that the kids were able to take advantage of me somewhat but they did well in their exams. The only sport I was any good at was long-distance running, though my legs were too short to reach the top in that field. And, with David, I have been doing a lot of sculpture quite proficiently. Maisie knows none of this, of course, so this is further evidence of her special talent.

I am aware that Socrates had fallen foul of the establishment and was forced to drink hemlock. "What part did I play in his demise?"

"You'd drifted away from the school by that time and avoided the political games that others played. You were aware of what was going on but chose to keep out of it - which your past life has regretted ever since. Draw Socrates close to you now." I try to but feel nothing.

"He is working around and supporting the current life from the Socrates source, incarnate in South Africa, where he is trying to make a difference in the politics there. You might be interested to know that your life after next will be a female politician, and your leader will again be from the Socrates line."

"In what country?", I ask, expecting it to be one of the important European ones.

"Corsica" is his response.

I let out a scathing "Corsica?!!"

Crito assures me that it is often best to do small things well rather than taking on an impossible task. "Would you like to be the leader of America today? Personally, I wouldn't recommend it."

Crito then informs me that this Greek life of mine will not be around me much in the future because of my lack of direct involvement in politics but, nevertheless, he is here at this sitting and assures me that he will work with me should the need arise.

The next day, I go to the library to research Socrates. Sure enough, Crito was one of the great man's closest companions. I also learned about the homosexual undercurrent in the elite of that time even though most of them were married. Clearly, my relationship with David is entirely a karmic one and the weight of the love we had in our past lives together is overriding his natural heterosexual nature enough for us to be together. Many of the Athenian men and the women, too, were bisexual. I need to know why.

Most of my past lives have been in a male yang body. This represents my essential nature. I am adventurous, always reaching out to expand my horizons with a warrior nature that I still like to express. The compliment to this is a yin sensitive, feminine, creative, embracing, nurturing and home-loving.

In our lives together, David has usually been in a female body. From his descriptions of them, all of his intimate relationships have been with strong yang woman. I ask Crito to explain this further.

"When you start your round of incarnations, this is in pairs, the yang man and the yin woman. This usually continues for several more lives by which time the two streams have usually become far too polarised. They are pigeonholed into fixed roles - the dominant male and the submissive, childbearing wife. So, by the fourth life, the female side wants to have some of the action and pressures the male side to swap. Yin man, yang woman."

This fits perfectly into what I have already been sensing. I contribute by adding that "further down the line, the yang side remains as it usually is, in a male body, and the yin soul also comes into a male body. That's what homosexuality is, not some aberrant urge."

"True, but they don't usually meet," Crito adds. "Then they wouldn't want to be with anyone else. So, they link up with people like their twin soul, and learn about each other in that way."

I butt in again with, "Of course, at some other time, the two halves incarnate as women who balance each other. The butch and the fem." Crito confirms this.

Two fingers up, then, to Mary Whitehouse, the evangelical Christian who is directing a crusade against the permissive society that I clearly belong to. It certainly explains my relationship with David much more deeply. Relationships and morality are much more complex than she understands.

To explore further, I regularly sit in tube carriages looking at couples opposite, trying to discern who wears the pants in that household. The man is often sitting, eyes closed, meditating, while the woman is looking around taking everything in.

I write down the characteristics that mark when they are in unfamiliar bodies. Bleached or brightly coloured hair, piercings, black leather, tattoos and tight or ripped jeans. Two of these and a crossover polarity is almost a certainty.

The feminist movement is run predominantly by yang women. Most actresses are yang. The composers, conductors and directors are mainly yin. I do a survey, assessing a hundred couples passing me in the street. I expect to find that around 80% are in unfamiliar bodies but, in London, it is much higher, around 93%. As a yang man, I am clearly an endangered species.

In the political field, Mrs Thatcher was a yang woman. Denis, her husband was definitely yin. That sex icon Marilyn Monroe was a yang woman. Now, that really challenges what sex appeal is. Her husband, the playwright Arthur Miller, was the creative yin. This is a fascinating study.

Crossover is necessary to achieve the balance lacking in the stream of lifetimes where karma has not been understood and worked out. Most problems arise with the yin men who convention says should be strong and assertive. If not, they must assume it.

Boxers are yin men, having to prove themselves. Many of our more ruthless leaders are obviously yin men. Cruelty is a part of their nature. The male concentration camp guards in WW2 were mainly yin. This, of course, created karma that would have to be resolved in later lives.

In ancient Greece, they developed a moral code where the men aspired to be the mythical hero and this was extended to loving the heroes in their midst. Many of these issues were worked on through their bisexuality. I spoke to Crito about this. He began by asking, "Why be defined by sexuality at all? In Ancient Greece, it was something that happened in the aristocracy, out of sight, and was seen as a natural thing. There were duties to perform but, other than that, we could do anything that felt good and, for many of us, being with a younger man was a valued experience."

"We believed that when our warriors loved each other, they would fight harder together. Quite a refreshing point of view."

"Issues only arose when the morals became overly rigid, as they did in Sparta where this archetype was taken to the limit. Perfection was the goal. Deformed babies were killed. Clashes often occurred when those following their impulses fell foul of the cultural norms."

"It became a militant society where the feminine was excluded, almost entirely. In marriage, the women mimicked a boy. This was rife with problems, but it was an effective way of organising society on another level."

"In Athens, there was considerable acceptance around that because the rigid power structures, that had been inherited from Egypt and their judgemental gods, needed to be relaxed. Some men, who were not the first or second born, could decide to pursue a different archetype, where they did not need to be with a woman at all. It was entirely permissible."

"In both sexes, people flexibly balanced their lives in ways appropriate to their human and spiritual needs, and why not? The women had their intimate involvement with other women by performing initiations, in the home, for those young women reaching adulthood, which the men knew nothing about."

"The exploration of bisexuality, in your own society, was inevitable because some of your homosexual lives, in earlier cultures, were treated appallingly, locked up or killed, and this has to be resolved. It can be quite complicated."

This is fairly reassuring but I want to know more about me. I point to my palm. "The destiny line tells me that I will marry and have a son. That is fine but, alongside, there is another line indicating that, some years later, I will meet a man who will, presumably, extend what is happening now with David."

Crito responds, "You are helping him to accept himself in this regard. It is an issue that you must work on with many people regardless of the outcome for you. When you fully allow this energy to flow, you will be what you need to be in all situations."

"What I am really wanting to know: Is my twin soul, in this present life, male or female?" I am already sensing the answer.

"Male. You are very much an old Athenian."

☙

David's art college year is over and I am looking forward to his homecoming. I am sublimely happy to see him when he arrives but he is awkward and unable to look me in the eyes. I reach down to take his bags upstairs when he says. "No, don't do that."

I turn to face him. He wants to say more but can't. His eyes turn to one side and then the other, for what seems like an eternity, before blurting out, "You are holding me back, Greg, holding me back. I have a job lined up at the Drill Hall," which is a squatted arts centre near Tottenham Court Road that we have both been involved in, "and I'm moving in with a group of artists there."

I am shaking my head in disbelief. He sees this and blurts out, "Greg, I'm leaving you." Then, after a long pause, "I can't stand this awful place any longer!"

I lead the way into the office. We sit down and say nothing for quite a while. My eyes are demanding an explanation, from anywhere. "Why!?" screams silently out of me.

"I wanted to break it to you gently," he eventually admits.

"I love you," I say quietly.

"I know. That's why I didn't just write you a letter. I owe you that, at least. I'll sleep down here tonight and be gone in the morning."

He obviously can't stand the intensity of my suppressed emotions and the hurt in my eyes. I go upstairs to the bedroom and lie down when the information I need floods in. I can see that he is a fellow student of Socrates.

In that life, too, we are deeply in love but I have a duty to perform, that comes first. I must take a journey with another man, who was a lover, years before, but now we are just good friends. This is too much for David's former life. It becomes a festering sore. He cannot believe that I have not betrayed him and paranoia sets in. He attempts to kill my friend. It is prevented but this leads to his rejection from Socrates' inner circle.

David and I have come together, so that all of the other more positive lives I have been contacting at night, while lying beside him, can come in and diffuse some of the negativity flowing in from this Greek life. It is clearly not enough.

I see David only once more - in Camden Market, a few weeks later. He notices me and walks the other way. I remind myself that I never cry when people part, only when they come together and are happy. So why am I sobbing now? Every night, for six months my pillow is soaked from my blubbering. Then suddenly it stops and I vow never to shed another tear for love, not ever, ever, ever again.

6

The Glastonbury adventure
1977

At the Warren Street squat, I've painted the downstairs room a brilliant white, to symbolise the purity otherwise lacking in my life, and bought a large purple rug in a car-boot sale. This is a perfect central location for 'The New Age Centre'. I advertise for therapists to work in our Saturday morning clinic. The only person to respond is Charles Sprung, formerly chief healer for Joe Benjamin, the popular cockney medium who drew large crowds locally to his demonstrations.

Once a month, Maisie's spirit guide, the Egyptian pharaoh Akhenaten, gives trance lectures following the healing. This attracts around a dozen regulars, so I decide to start up a 'Saturday Forum' where well-known speakers in the psychic and natural therapy fields can pass on their understanding."

Later, we turn one of the basement rooms into a yoga and exercise space. This inspires Maisie to channel a comprehensive set of spiritual movement exercises drawing on higher energies and concepts which she calls Florette.

During my time in England, I've not strayed far from London, but I am feeling a pull to rectify that. "The Glorious and Magical 7-7-77 Glastonbury Fayre" is coming up but I know that isn't for me. My camping out in mud days are long over but this seems to be the right direction to follow.

I mention this to Maisie who responds casually, "Oh, it is part of your search for the Holy Grail." My ignorance once again exposed, it is back to the library where I learn that the Holy Grail is one of the most enduring legends in Western European literature and art.

Said to be the cup of the Last Supper and, at the Crucifixion, to have received blood flowing from Christ's side. Do I believe it? Not a scrap.

Faced with conflicting versions aplenty, I settle on the idea that it was brought to Britain by Joseph of Arimathea, where it has lain hidden ever since. So, who was this Joseph? One story goes that he was related to Jesus, perhaps an uncle, who brought the young lad to Glastonbury. When he set his walking staff on the ground, it miraculously took root, leafed out, and blossomed as the "Glastonbury Thorn." It has continued to flower twice a year, in winter and spring, ever since.

Word of that got around and the story was kept alive over the centuries, as miracles were always good for the pilgrim trade which flourished at Glaston until the Abbey was dissolved in 1539 during the English Reformation.

"We must go there," I insist, "We can take a van, a group of us, and tour the area.

"That will have to be with your friends," Maisie responds, "I was there during the war and my guides are telling me that I don't need to go again."

Not satisfied with this, I raise it with her guide, Feca. "You must realise that she is an old lady with unreliable waterworks. She doesn't feel comfortable with this kind of upheaval at her age but yes, we want her to go with you."

This isn't the first time the guides have contradicted her beliefs. Indeed, it is the main thing that confirms her integrity. To be conscious and let through information that you don't personally believe is a very mature spiritual ability.

I put the word around to the members of my growing

circle of seekers and there is great enthusiasm for a chance to get away. That summer, eight of us pack into a van and, for three days, tour the West Country, clearing away karmic dross from various historical sites, some of it very cruel indeed, and reinvigorating the energies there, before arriving in Glastonbury.

We did not book ahead. In those days, it was very easy to just stop along the way when you saw a sign up. On this occasion, the tourist office checks us into the Ashwell Lane digs run by Mrs Parfitt, on the far side of the Tor. She is very sympathetic to our work and directs us to the various sites.

Apart from the many new age diversions we encounter, the people of Glastonbury live firmly in the past, resentful that the Pilton rock festival is so close. It is just finishing as we arrive. The "No Hippies" signs, on many trees, alert us to their concerns.

On visiting St John's church on the high street, we need to knock. A prim and very nervous woman peers around the door at us. "Thank God", she says, "it is so difficult keeping those young people out." If she knew what we are really up to, she would be holding up a cross and, with a "Get thee hence, Satan", we would be repelled back into the sinful world outside that is relentlessly encroaching on their purity.

I have read about the fate of Glastonbury Abbey when Henry the Eighth's anti-catholic purgers arrived in town. Abbot Whiting and two of his monks were taken to the nearby Tor and nailed to crosses. In the crypt, Richard Whiting speaks through Maisie. He asks us to help him down from his cross.

"Jesus has been up there longer than me", he bemoans. If only the church would understand redemption better and the need to go beyond the past." He accepts our healing, but it can only be partial at this time. He is locked into the spiritual karma of Glastonbury in very complex ways, and there is much re-awakening of that energy still to take place before he will be free.

With my mathematical background, I am aware that the structure of the Abbey is influenced by the occult numerology enshrined there. Numbers have a great significance - and when a certain number is entered into by any company of people, the significance is released.

In the crypt, a communicator, speaking through Maisie, tells us that there were once twelve monks in residence, all adepts filled with the Christ power. They practiced higher occultism and performed many healing miracles. I feel them around us still influencing events from the spirit world and, with many others, using the prayers and the devotion of the faithful on Earth as a catalyst for change.

The laity did not know about any of this, of course, but the monasteries all had their occult circles. Some monks were in communion with the advanced ones in spirit who came to guide and direct. But, later, this monastery became rife with gluttony and very catholic kinds of debauchery. Some had their concubines and depravity took hold, but oh so cleverly hidden.

They often went on pilgrimages to get away from the discipline of the monastery. In the Abbey, there was the holy and the unholy. So, when dissolution was dispatched there, it was a dreadful time, but not totally unjust.

Many monks defected and linked up with the marauders who promised them immunity. But did they give it? Oh, no. And there were those who tried to hold onto the valuables, some of which, I sense, are still hidden in the earth and will come to light eventually. Most, however, could not bear the torture and they revealed the hiding places before they were executed.

Despite the terror, the more courageous brethren met in secret. No one could hold the Christ spirit back. When these awful events were over, many signs were given to them that the time would come when the Glastonbury area would once again be a seat of great power, of great wisdom.

We solemnly walk the length of the ruins to the high

altar and then across to the monks' quarters. When Maisie visited the Abbey grounds previously she was drawn to the 'Abbot's kitchen', the only building still intact, where she was confronted by sinister hooded figures, revolting creatures that she managed to release into the light, all except one. And here he is now, as we enter, desperately crying out for help.

Black magic was practised by some of the inner coterie of monks, "including me," he admits with immense sorrow. We form a circle and lift him out of his mental trap, sending him gratefully on his way.

This was quite intense work, so we decide to take time off to reflect on what we've experienced. I come across a sign marking the supposed final resting place of the Camelot couple, King Arthur and Guinevere, but my scepticism hurries me on by.

On reaching the fish pond, I lie down and turn my mind back to events that happened after the destruction of the Abbey. I can feel one of the twelve adepts in spirit positioning himself beside me, a jovial chap. He confirms that the attack on their religious community had been an unfortunate necessity. It was an attempt to free the area from the control of the Church but the Church elders did not take the hint. They went on asserting the importance of Glaston as a Christian site and it has remained a point of pilgrimage for both the Anglican and Roman Catholic clergy ever since.

Every year, they and their people assemble at the Abbey ruins at exactly the same time, each holding their ceremonies but, within a locked religious tradition they cannot enter into the true significance of what needs to be achieved here.

"They have helped keep the energy in a cage" and I can feel a great sadness coming from him as he says, "The Church hierarchies, alas, still do not accept that they are only doorkeepers at the house of the Lord, not its owner."

His final words are more positive. "The Abbey is no longer deeply troubled. Much work has been done, over the decades, by a few devoted groups who use the subtle energies to clear obstructions and move things forward. At the completion of this mission to Glaston, many people will attend a service of thanksgiving here at the Abbey. They will be able to see us and their own past lives. It will be a joyous occasion."

The following day, our landlady takes us to meet Christine Jagg, who lives diagonally opposite her on Ashwell Lane, an immensely warm and welcoming figure in her late seventies. She and her companion sit us down to a feast of delicious homemade cakes before giving us the largely forgotten history of the area. Christine is the only surviving member of the Company of Twelve, a mediumistically based group of seekers.

She gives us the last copies of their books, full of archaic language, diagrams and alchemical charts, but the most interesting part of her story is about the three groups in Glastonbury who used various rituals during the war to send out streams of uncompromising thought energy to stop Hitler in his tracks. In addition to her own group, there was Dion Fortune's band of occultists and a very important circle organised by Wellesley Tudor Pole, who lived in the Chalice Well house.

"The Chalice Well is easily the most enchanted spot in town, nestled beneath the troubled Tor rising majestically above it. Go to the Upper Room where they met," she advises, "and Wellesley's spirit will be there to greet you".

Tudor Pole was a confidant of Churchill, and he encouraged the great man to instigate the silent minute when, at 9 pm, on hearing the chimes of Big Ben on the radio, the whole country stood and prayed for peace. It was believed, by many people at the time, that this turned the tide of the war against the Germans.

This Upper Room has been recently divided into two parts, separated by a gauze curtain through which we can see a table with thirteen chairs set up as the last supper and, in the window, a candle. There is a circle of chairs for our quiet meditation time. Talking is forbidden, a sign on the door informs us, but that doesn't expressly include spirits so we light our own candle in the middle of our circle, and wait for Tudor Pole to speak.

"You have come to this important place, to help us anchor what you are doing for us, deep into the earth, so that our influence can extend further out into your world. I tried not to impose any fixed belief on this room. It is a pity that others have done so since. Many people come here and only look to the light. They do not ground their energies. I know you understand this."

"You have expressed interest in the Holy Grail which, you need to know, is not a physical artefact. There is no cup nor parchment nor shrine for you to find. It contains your personal structure of power and intention that links up with those in our world who share your mission. It is your source reality and includes all defining experiences that brought you to the present moment, to be integrated and celebrated now in the great hall of eternity."

"The link is particularly potent in this sanctuary because of all the fine enactments at the well, throughout the ages, especially the healing miracles. We are assisting you to chip away the encrustations of the past holding you down, holding you back. The light can only shine in when the windows of your soul are open. In this sanctuary, we helped achieve peace in a troubled world that has, alas, remained resolutely at war ever since. So, I am inviting you to join me in a meditation for lasting peace." This we did. His final words were the most meaningful.

"To liberate this land from the oppressors who would enslave humanity, by leading you into the clutches of materialism, there is only one way, to enter fully into the heart where you will discover your divine self. A simple concept, taught by the great masters, and the one most difficult to implement. It is about achieving balance when faced with a deceptive external world that encourages division and conflict. From there, send roots down deep into the earth, as an oak, a willow, or an ancient yew, whichever is your kind of tree, so that you can stand firm and inspire the world as you are meant to do. Go in joy, my friends, with all our gratitude and love."

So, I have come all this way to discover that my search for the grail is an inner one, after all. I look out of a window into the beautiful well garden below, which is shining with a light I've not seen previously. I am reminded that the outer reality still offers many transcendent delights when we are ready to engage with them.

Out in the gardens, the incredibly pure radiations flow into me. We lift the cover protecting the well but it is hard to see the water through the moss and the shade. We stand around it and meditate. I am tuning into the healing waters that have been flowing for many long centuries, cleansing and clearing, and I remember my duty as a child of nature to allow the healing properties to flow through me.

Although this is effectively launching my work as a healer, I am aware that I have to first eradicate some of the dark and muddied waters within myself, before I can get to the causes of ill-health in other people.

I ask Maisie to delve more deeply into the history of the well. Reminders of the Christian heritage are everywhere but the legends need to be tested. A spirit communicator announces himself as one of the 27 disciples that Jesus sent to build the first church in England, very near to where we are standing, but 18, including himself, were killed by hostile locals. This is where Christianity first put down roots and where it had its first major setback.

The water is piped down to a level below the well where we can drink it. I gulp down six glasses in a row determined to get as much of the blessed stuff into me as I can. A bit excessive really. I have realised that taking in such water brings the influence of the blood of many martyrs with it, those strong persecuted souls who held on because of the light of the Christ energy in their hearts, who felt loyalty to those messengers of the past, whose work they knew they were carrying forward.

The Chalice Well has been a great baptismal font, much

larger than it is now. Wellesley, speaking to me inwardly now, confides that the remaining disciples trained a team of healers to carry forward their mission. Many people, crippled or infirm, were able to stand and walk after emerging from the water. A strong tradition of healing was developed here and all who can enter into that mystical element of the spirit will realise that the healing waters do not flow just for the body, but for the mind and the soul as well.

I don't identify as Christian, in any religious sense, but these cleansing, revitalising waters of spirit are usually associated with the healing power of the Christ energy. I must learn how to direct this power, that is surging through me now, into those who come to me for healing.

We pass many who are meditating quietly in the Well gardens, withdrawing from the harsher elements today and tuning in to the nature spirits here. They know that spiritual energy is not engaged with by force, control, exclusivity, or any of the over-the-top approaches found elsewhere in Glastonbury but, on talking to several of them, they don't seem to understand that practical input from another level is an essential part of detachment.

It is time for our trek up the Tor, stopping at Dion Fortune's former cottage on the way where we have arranged to meet the new owner, Geoffrey Ashe, the noted spiritual historian. From there, we do not take the quickest route, straight up, because Maisie isn't too steady on her pins. We stop many times to adjust to the energies and admire the view. I can feel that, while the Abbey generates the power and the Well dispenses it through the faithful, the Tor is a beacon for the world to navigate by.

In former days, the Tor enhanced the healing process. Taking the energies they'd received at the Chalice Well, those who could, proceeded up to the Church of St Michael at the top where the healing was augmented within them; and they passed these enhanced energies down to the many who could not go beyond the foot of the Tor because of their afflictions.

Too many of those who climb the Tor today are thrill-seekers. As we walk slowly up, we are passed by dozens of young people surging up the slope. On reaching the summit, I am immediately uplifted. It is a bit intoxicating but these are very mixed vibrations. Discordant streams of energy are coming in and clashing. Some are linked to persecutions and conflicts worldwide. We spend a full half-hour linking into our hearts and projecting the energy of the Tor to the Chalice Well and then to the Abbey. We are learning how to become an integral part of the transformation process.

Maisie tells us that she is aware of only three other groups involved in developing the Tor energies on the level we are working on. One of these was here recently and we decide to carry on with what they had been doing, strengthening the neglected link to the fish-like Wearyall Hill with its holy thorn. We must be careful to keep out intrusions from the shadow ones who wish to corrupt the energies there.

The Tor is linked to the Cosmos, but I can't seem to extend up that far because the power available, though still strong here, is retreating to a smaller sphere of consciousness. Even so, Glaston remains one of the great power emanations, linking up strongly with centres in the Himalayas and the Gobi desert, where some of the energy released during the nuclear period is being harnessed to build stable global energy structures needed for the Aquarian age.

Because Glaston is essentially a third eye chakra energy, many who come here are prone to fantasy. While exploring the high street, later that day, we are approached by people who are misusing the psychic gifts, all trying to lure us into their clutches. At the Assembly Rooms, we meet up with a group of witches, white ones, they assure us, who invite Maisie to their rituals. Declined. At this time, the new age bandwagon has not yet fully arrived, but preparations are going on for an eventual takeover.

1978

We have successfully set up the Warren Street squat as a fairly respectable therapy centre by advertising widely. Our healing clinic is well attended and my development as a healer is proceeding slowly but surely. Maisie is sceptical about formal training. Her one instruction is, "Just put your hands on the shoulders of as many people that will let you and in six years you'll be a healer."

"Six years," I'd impatiently thought. "surely there is a quicker way." With that in mind, I am developing a special breathing process where I inhale fully, pause, then very slowly breathe out through the nose, extending this out-breath further than I feel comfortable with.

After three full breaths, there is a tingling in my fingers with the psychic breezes wafting over them. Then, I sense higher energies descending and lower ones rising to meet harmoniously in my heart. I must always encourage my client to do this breathing also so that we can be in sync. That was it. My learning couldn't have been more effortless.

Fortunately, one of the people who has joined my development circle is a biofeedback machine operator and we are planning some research into the brainwave patterns of healers and their clients during the healing process.

It is exciting work. Despite being very wary of the electrodes we need to place on her head, Maisie agrees to participate. I am the patient for her. Our brainwave patterns are entirely different when we start but after I do my breathing technique there is great jubilation around me. My patterns have become exactly the same as hers.

I had always thought, as many healers do, that power goes into the patient through both hands but this is unbalanced and the healing is blocked. The machine shows that one hand directs the healing in to a precise point within the condition while the other draws the disturbed energies out from there.

To become more involved in the healing fraternity, I join the Federation of Spiritual Healers and am soon voted in as the chairperson of the London steering committee. Before I get too swollen-headed, they tell me that this is because no one else wants that responsibility.

Our average age is over sixty. I am easily the youngest. All of them started developing their gift after their children had left home and they had the time to commit to it.

Watching our senior healer, Charles, do his routine, I realise that older people are much slower, and this is an essential attribute for a healer. He has a stream of clients who come week after week but very few people return for another dose of my healing. This is quite damaging to my confidence. I ask Maisie to explain why.

Her response is "No more than 10% of the NFSH members are true healers. The rest work near the surface, integrating the energies and comforting the clients, which is useful, but they don't go deep enough into the condition to get at the cause. By penetrating precisely into the patient's condition, you tend to disturb the more suppressed karmic energies and few people want to go through that, so they back away until they are ready to face those issues."

Yes, I do want to explore the frontiers of healing and many other areas of psychic expression - that is my nature – but it doesn't bring in the crowds.

1979

Summer is approaching and it is time to return to Glastonbury. One of my close but awkward friends, Peter Woodcock, has moved there and promises to enthuse our group around the secret places in the surrounding hamlets. We settle into Mrs Parfitt's digs and, the next morning, meet up with Peter in the centre of town. It is the second weekend in July when the church pilgrimages to the Abbey take place. We are heavily outnumbered.

There is still work to be done in the crypt beneath the Lady Chapel, so we wait with heads bowed till the Anglican chappie has finished his blessing. We are left alone by the other adult visitors but, after sitting down in the altar area to begin meditating, a group of young kids start throwing pebbles at us from the lookout platform above. The shadow spirits are using impressionable young minds to get at us, but we keep going.

The monks of old, who stayed on to move the energy forward, are clearly glad to see us. Our presence seems to be much more compatible with their needs than the competing ceremonies dotted around the grounds. One monk, speaking through Maisie, tells us how to direct energy to assist them with their clearing work. He wants us to think of Jesus on the cross while we work, which I don't find easy. It is a very unbalanced cross.

A visit to the Abbot's kitchen completes our itinerary. No negative energies remain there, thanks to our earlier work, but we are called on to give some healing to a very distressed elderly woman who has been overwhelmed by the proceedings. We play the role of Christian healers very convincingly and she responds well.

We then move on to the magical Chalice Well House and climb the stairs to the Upper Room eager to hear more from its particularly gifted custodian, Wellesley Tudor Pole, speaking again through Maisie from beyond the beyond.

He encourages us to enter into the silence and commune with the masters. "In this Centre of Light, let inspiration flow. We bring thanks to you who are ready to take up the subtle threads of truth and weave them into a practical philosophy that gives compelling reasons for any true seeker to obey the laws and teachings of the great ones." He then instructs us how to draw the energies of Glaston more fully into our hearts.

Wellesley was an inspired channel but he did not complete his mission because of the restrictions of his time and the lack of people able to work on his level of spiritual maturity.

"Although the Christ energy is still influential here, it is not always channelled into the right procedures that will integrate the old and the new ways of working with the natural order - always supported by the elementals and the devas. Once there was a harmonious link between the Abbey, the Chalice Well and the Tor, a triumvirate of energies that inspired many open-hearted pilgrims to visit and participate. Not so many come today."

"People are much more self-centred and do not use the energies here to resolve the gross things, enacted over the centuries, that are still embedded in the earth all around this region. We need human channels who have done the necessary preparation to effectively direct transformative energies through them, but few are ready for that responsibility."

He speaks again of the blood that is circulating freely, carrying the messages of the Godhead which inspire all those who seek to promulgate the truth. "It is like the waters of life that the master spoke about, but they need to flow into dual streams of expression merging again in a purified condition to assert a positive influence on the world."

He then tells us that there are two springs, the red, iron-based one we know, feminine and nurturing and the, little recognised, white, masculine, calcium one located outside the Well enclosure which is precisely linked to all the energy points in the Glaston area. "It will be quite a while before the white spring is fully integrated into the rituals and processes of those working for the overall wellbeing of Glastonbury."

"The Chalice Well still has many healing properties available for individuals, but the higher ministry of healing is needed now. Good people must open up to the quickening power more fully, so that the redemptive energies can be directed towards the disruptive forces operating worldwide. Many souls, visiting the Well gardens through the ages, have left their healing thoughts in the atmosphere. These need to be re-contacted and merged so that this intercessory process can be more fully mobilised."

The venerable old yew tree shading the lower well area also speaks through Maisie bemoaning the fact that he wants to die but the human stewards there see him as a vital part of the fabric of the gardens. So, he keeps going due to popular demand. We give him a hug.

Of course, we are not regular visitors, and Wellesley needs people on the spot able to help him attract out the subtle transformative energies that flow through the waters here. While there are still a few working quietly in the background who can harness some of the remaining miracle-working power, more need to link up with Wellesley Tudor-Pole now, so that the revivification of the whole well energy can be completed.

We spend several days visiting the surrounding hamlets ending up just outside the ten-mile Glastonbury circle where we walk up a steep incline to visit Cadbury Castle. It is a raised flattish surface with nothing to indicate any building or former community but Maisie knows exactly where to go to make contact with the past.

It is reputed to have been the home of King Arthur but how genuine is this? Maisie channels figures from the past, and the first to come through is a rather sad individual who identifies himself as King Uther.

According to the myths, he was Arthur's father but these are amalgamations of events over long periods of time, added to and modified by each succeeding generation. "My earth life was thousands of years before Arthur. I led my people following the destruction of Atlantis, but I failed completely", he laments with a hissing sigh. "I was too influenced by those around me. They wanted to carry on the old traditions, but it was these practices that brought that civilisation down."

"They wanted us to reach out more into the surrounding settlements but I knew it was too early to share what we knew with others. I should have asserted my authority more because things started to go disastrously astray. There were many out there only too eager to do battle with us. I died a very painful and unnecessary death."

The next chap, bemoaning the coming of the Romans into Britain, tells us that the natural spiritual energies found in Glastonbury soon retreated to Cornwall where they were gradually directed deep into the earth to prevent them from being corrupted by the invaders.

This is why there is little of the old Celtic consciousness alive in England today though some people in the West country, with direct genetic links to the early ones, are beginning to liberate these energies once more.

Uther tried to give reality to a few of the more fantastical elements. He told us that "There were many Arthurs over the centuries who were part of that very special line of evolution that has ingrained itself in the consciousness of this country."

They are all grateful to us for listening to their stories but none of these fits into the historical timeline I am working to.

The final communicator comes with a special request to ask Merlin to visit them should we meet up with him on our travels. "It's been over a thousand years since he was last here."

My unexpected response is, "He came with us. Can't you see him?"

"Oh, yes. So, he is. Thank you on behalf of us all – and do return soon."

It will be several years before we comply and another fifteen before I put aside my deep scepticism to seriously investigate the real events behind these legendary tales and how they relate to the present.

7

When the Dark and Light embrace

1981

Marriage is on my mind. My palm says that this should have happened by now. So, where is she? Maisie confirms that it is time to start the search but she is reluctant to give any more detail. It's up to me then. Thanks, Maisie.

I am not a natural meditator. In trying to focus on the truth, I become becalmed in the head. This is a heart matter. I am slowing down my breathing and she is coming into focus. Slim. I prefer that, with dark hair and quite attractive. She comes from a wealthy family and is a daughter of the Swiss Ambassador to – somewhere. Ah yes, the US of A and she is living in New York City. I immediately pack my bags.

Once there, I rent a room in Greenwich Village with a woman who invites spiritual teachers to run weekend groups in her spacious apartment. I attend them all and then range out to visit many therapy and new age centres around. Wainwright House and the Temple of Understanding in Rye are particularly interesting to me. I am soon totally immersed in the lively spiritual scene, making many friends and having a wonderful time - but no future wife appears. I hardly notice.

Several trips later, I attend a trance group session with, the well-regarded, Alexander Murray. One of the other sitters is a very enthusiastic, very arty, very masculine and very outspoken lesbian from a downtown arts centre. She seems reluctant to speak to me.

Back home, when describing my exploits to Maisie, I suddenly realise that the woman I am meant to marry, was intending to accompany that one to the group but, at the last minute, chose not to. Maisie is now willing to discuss this with me.

"On the inner levels, she decided not to marry you, Greg. That's why she didn't appear. She would have had to come to this country with you and settle down. She is just not willing to leave the exciting life there to fulfil her destiny in your arms."

"Oh, well, her loss," I retort, flipping her out of my reality. Then I remember that my palm says that another person, male probably, will appear later to take over from her. When will this be? Will he be my twin soul? Maisie assures me that he will definitely be my true affinity in this life.

I close my eyes, and there he is. Taller than me. Brown wavy hair, thinning, and with glasses. An excellent musician. Totally involved in the nightlife. Drinks a bit too much. A great zest for life, but harbouring a deep sadness underneath. One of his best friends has died quite recently. Drugs, probably.

I am inwardly reminded that it is very rare for the twin souls to meet in any life. However, in our case, it is vital. The female line of incarnation, directly complementing mine, has fallen behind in evolution and we are coming together to try to lift him up into a closer alignment with me. The guides think that I am strong and detached enough to do this. So, back to New York and quite a different search.

I have kept away from the seedier areas, especially the many dives on the notorious Christopher Street and those on West Street, near the river, but that's where I'm drawn now. There have been a few shootings around here, and it's still quite dangerous. I know that I am protected and don't feel in any way vulnerable. I follow other leads but these are equally unsuccessful

I return later that year, determined to find this elusive chap but, by then, the AIDS crisis has hit the city hard and everyone is frightened. Not me, of course. I know that only the experiences I need for my spiritual growth will come to me.

Many community groups have been set up to support those affected and I visit every one in my search for my musician counterpart. I am staying with a friend near the Brooklyn Bridge who encourages me to become an activist again. I march beside him down Fifth Avenue holding a very provocative placard. The cheers far outnumber the boos as we pass.

Several months after returning to London and a few hours into a restless night, I suddenly become aware of a car negotiating a mountain road in upper New York State, which screeches out of control and crashes into a ravine. No one could survive that.

A shattering dissolution of my energies follows. I know immediately that it is my twin soul down there, crushed out of life. Was he running away from me?

I won't look out for any newspaper reports of this. There is no need. Without a doubt, he is gone. We will not meet our destined rendezvous in this life and the detachment I feel from my feminine side can never be fully resolved.

1987

Western religions have distorted and misrepresented the teachings of Jesus and are still unwilling to unpick their many early doctrinal errors that have been so detrimental to human progress. These were systematically extended by the Popes and their advisors to control the masses. The amount of guilt and shame lodged in their loyal followers relegated them to being 'miserable sinners', rather than noble missionaries on a shared evolutionary path.

So, under Maisie's guidance, I probe back into my past where I contact a number of lives in Catholic countries who secretly disobeyed the dictates of the 'Holy Fathers'. In one, I met with other heretics in underground caves where we worshipped the primitive gods. I can hear the drums echoing into the bowels of the earth and, even today, the thought of this sends a thrill through me. I stood up to their wrong thinking, with a reckless disregard for the inevitable backlash, and was knocked down again and again.

It didn't start well for me in the second century when some church leaders, in their zeal to draw people in, abandoned the simple teachings of their master. They said that those who did not convert to their version of His teachings would not merely die, they would be thrown into an eternal fire. Their beliefs were based on pagan descriptions of hell which, of course, had no biblical basis. I pointed this out and became an outcast.

Moving forward to a significant life around 325 A.D. when the Catholic church had evolved into an institution ripe for manipulation. By now, the Church-State alliance had the sole purpose of achieving blind-faith dependence on them by the masses. So, under Emperor Constantine, the Nicaean Council declared that Jesus was a part of God, the Son aspect of the trinity, and that the rest of the human flock are, and must remain, separate from their Source.

Like many early Christians, I believed that every soul descends from heaven to live by the teachings of the Master, returning there a better person at the end. Pre-incarnation consciousness was a widely held Christian belief until 553 A.D when the more ambitious church elders, who wanted the people to feel and not think, took the upper hand at the Fifth Ecumenical Council of Constantinople convened by Emperor Justinian.

A total of 15 Anathemas, or condemnations, were enacted; the first being, "If anyone assert the fabulous pre-existence of the souls, and shall assert monstrous restoration which follows from it, let him be an anathema." From that point on, priests who taught pre-incarnation were ruthlessly persecuted, including that former life of mine.

Maisie is a very accomplished past life therapist and she has seen that our destiny paths had come together often in earlier times, but usually on opposite sides. She did not start rebelling against the false doctrines until later when she realised that the belief that God created every one of us individually at the moment of conception, was a most pernicious error. This blocks the full evolutionary energy streaming through from the past. Christians were reduced to approaching infinity from one direction only, instead of precisely balancing the past and the future in the eternal now.

I accept that Jesus was one of the great ones to walk this planet, teaching that we are all sons and daughters of God and there is no separation. One of my past lives is still forcefully proclaiming, "Jesus did not have a virgin birth! His mission was to demonstrate a simple humanness and that would have made him super-human from the start. You tell me that if I don't repent and lead a righteous life, to your specifications, I will be banished to hell forever. I am not wicked by nature. There is no hell, except in your own self-satisfied minds." No wonder Pope Innocent had him put to death.

Apparently, there was a point in the sixteenth century when Maisie finally agreed, "What a load of rubbish" and, from then on, we have been compatriots in the quest for truth.

Despite her knowing that any belief where the light dominates and excludes the dark is just as unfortunate as the other way round, her Christian position has certainly been influenced by the image of Akhenaten welcoming the rays of light from above.

She still relegates the earth aspect of the Mother to an inferior position in the murky underworld, as the patriarchal Christian leaders did.

I can hear one of her former male lives, who wanted me to join them in their crusade to reform religion. "Get thee behind me Satan, is false", he is saying. "It keeps past sins firmly unresolved in the past." True, but the most powerful karmic challenges "hide and fester below us, in Hades", as the Greeks depicted it. Satan is down there, too, but what about Mrs Satan? What is She up to? One day, I will go down into their realm and make peace with both of Them.

Maisie is aware that I am delving into the subterranean worlds, and decides, "It's time to step up your training, Greg, to face much more serious challenges."

That sounds ominous even to a newly emboldened adventurer like me. I have helped her clear ghosts from gloomy places and confronted mischievous spirits causing trouble. What could be more serious than that? I wait for her to continue but she takes her time.

"Wickedness", comes eventually, with a twinkle in her eye. "The really bad guys. The dark forces, plotting and planning to get more power and they'll want to take it from you."

"Dark?", I counter, "I like the dark now."

"Yes. It is the wrong word", she accepts. "I meant 'the shadow band', those malevolent spirits who come around people in positions of authority, whispering how marvellous they are and leading them to enact policies that do not serve the greater good. You'll have to stand up to them and that requires a high degree of trust in your spirit guides when you venture into the forlorn places in the earth, where I cannot go."

"How can you guarantee that I'll be safe down there?", I protest.

She smiles, "Oh, stop being a namby, Greg. I wouldn't suggest something you can't do" and, after making eye contact, "Don't worry, I'll show you how to face their nonsense without being in any danger."

I have often marvelled at Maisie's composure. The psychic experience is all very matter-of-fact to her. No unnecessary Hollywood dramatics.

Just a very intense inner focus and a stillness that radiates out from her when she is working.

"The secret is that you mustn't engage with them until they are in a weakened position. They have been on a bad path far longer than you have been treading the good. So, be sneakier than they are. Put up smoke screens to keep them guessing. That's what the guides do."

How can I learn to face evil without needing to construct massive auric defences? "Balance," Maisie tells me, "and a precise inner focus." Light and dark are not synonymous with good and evil, I know that already. The light can be used for both good and ill, the dark, too. Wickedness then, why not?

I know Maisie to be a very tough yin woman but, when I begin my psychic resilience training, I realise that I am being required to ground her experiences and abilities. At times, she asks me to replace her husband in that work. We are complementing each other.

Together, we have already dealt with old evil, the residues of past blunders locked into historic buildings and sites, but I now I must face what lies behind the even more dangerous present evil, flooding the world through the actions of leaders who are in the thrall of the shadow spirits with their persuasive and very devious enticements.

"There is a really reprehensible character there, brought to us by the guides. He is trying to drum up racial hatred and wants to stop you interfering." The form of a man immediately appears to the right of me, and behind him is a Mosque. "You can see that he is up to no good and wants to keep you wrong-footed."

"On the spirit side, these baddies usually work in groups with one or two dominant ones sucking energy out of their followers, so that they can carry out their nefarious work. Do not engage with him directly."

I have no intention of doing that. He is a really nasty piece of work.

"When these past entities are not willing to co-operate

and stay linked up with the more treacherous spirit minds who control them, the shadow band, we can achieve little. So, start by inviting one of his acolytes forward."

I focus on this. There are two.

"Two, yes," Maisie confirms. "Now, place one of them within your safe space. He seems eager to escape from his 'master'. Stay inwardly focussed and breathe deeply. I will draw in the other one. Don't let impatience get the better of you, just stay still and the links they have to their boss will dissolve, eventually."

I instinctively slow down and focus in my heart as the secure place to work from. Getting into a balanced position is the essential first step.

"When the dualities are in harmony, no negativity can intrude. As with people, many spirits are defensive when challenged and this aggravates things if you engage with them."

"Don't worry," I assure her. "I won't fall into that trap."

"Invite this minion to join you in the present moment, where he certainly won't want to be, but needs to be, and trust that he will respond."

"He's there," I mutter, though not entirely sure.

"The next step will take time. Feel what is going on with him. Slow down more into your heart and he might be willing to follow you there."

I register a hatred extending back to a Persian life when the English invaded. To address this, I place a point midway between us and mentally step up to it, inviting him to join me.

I hold myself very still, breathing deeply and slowly, cautiously expectant and to shaking a bit to release the tension built up during this waiting period. Then my aura seems to shudder. I have attracted some energies that definitely aren't mine and I must let go of them. I then send thoughts of encouragement to this subservient soul but a little of my own energy goes with it.

Maisie senses this. "Don't give your power away. It is a serious error. The energy that releases must flow around you, through you, but not from you." I immediately stop and detach. There is a sudden release and I know that both of these acolytes will soon be free.

"Now, I will tackle the ringleader. You can support me." She lifts up a wooden cross plucked from her handbag. "Focus your mind into this," she demands of the spirit. "It is time you learnt the error of your ways."

I am entirely caught up in Maisie's formidable strength. I have worked beside her many times and still marvel at her steely gaze and indomitable will. But this is the first time I am expected to play a full balancing role. I emphasise her words in my mind, "the error of your ways." He can't get at me. I am sure of that.

"All done", she announces. "He'll do no more harm now. That he came at all indicated that he would be ready to release once his support was taken away." Though quite dramatic, this was an easy job for us. Other, more devious spirits, will be far more difficult to dislodge later.

Maisie informs me that this was a past life of one of her clients who had been hearing voices that were telling her to do quite awful things. "She's been coming to my healing clinic for months but fear always got in the way." We've had to work remotely to resolve it but," Maisie warns, "this will not end it. Other lives, with similar issues, will come forward now to drag her down again."

We do 'Spirit Release', she stresses, "I am not an exorcist. The difference becomes clear when I learn that an Anglican vicar and his wife do exorcisms in a North London church. I write to them and, several days later, I receive their ornately penned reply on church notepaper, inviting us both to attend their next session.

Maisie knows what to expect. It is the usual "Leave this person, wicked spirit. Out!," kind of thing. Several followers rock backwards and forwards chanting, "Out evil spirit. Out evil spirit." The vicar shouts, pointing towards the earth. "Get thee to Hell where you belong."

Maisie whispers to me, "Oh, my God, the poor thing."

"The spirit or the person?"

"Both", she replies, much more loudly.

"Shhh!," says someone nearby, "Have respect."

We eventually can't stand any more of this and leave conspicuously. Once outside, Maisie cannot contain herself. "How on earth can that young woman live with herself after that travesty. Jesus taught that love overcomes evil. Where was the love there?"

"Should we tell them?"

"No, they won't listen."

We go to a nearby park and sit on a bench. "I must bring that spirit through me. He's more confused and angry now than he was before." She closes her eyes and, for the first time, I can see who is there. I am even able to feel what he is going through.

"What's up, mate?", I say.

"I want her to love me, but she won't. I'm not going to give up."

"You must leave her alone. You can't force love. Go to your heart, now, and find peace."

"My heart is in pain".

"Deeper than that. Slow down." I raise my hands, with the palms directing healing towards his heart. Gradually, his distress is relieved.

"It is as simple as that," Maisie says when she comes out of trance. "Oh, when will these religious fools start realising that very little of this is actually evil and it must never be a battle. Hell is inside the exorcists – more often than not."

"When people pass on, any negative karma, left behind, can only be addressed on the human level, so we must work with the incarnate one to resolve the issues. These former lives can only come as near as we allow them to. Spiritual discipline is vital so that everything is regulated and manageable. Otherwise, over-assertive past personalities can come too close and bother us with their demands. Sometimes, there is a ruthlessness or insanity there and, if this intrudes too much, a situation develops that the church sees as possession."

Religions tell us to concentrate on the Father aspect of the Godhead. They don't want us to go down to the Earth Mother to achieve balance. There is usually a lot of negative past stuff waiting down there. Many people suppress it when it begins to rise up, vowing to never go near it again. They energetically poise their centre of gravity above the heart and out of range of the past's influence and benefits. Then, it is easy for them to abuse Gaia mercilessly.

Most moral degradation stems from fear of what lies in the earth which is translated into a fear of 'the evil other'. Difference is demonised. It has allowed atrocities to proliferate in the Middle East and it has become politically incorrect to speak out when some minorities in this country behave badly.

We, comfortable Westerners, are immensely conflicted about these matters, reluctant to act decisively to address the contradictions and counter such thinking. We are, to a greater or lesser extent, slaves to our own unreasoning minds and unwilling to make sense of the inconsistencies lower down.

Most people today have forgotten that the still heart rules, or should, not the intellect. As I further develop my yang healing, I am learning how to breathe the higher into the lower and the lower into the higher, simultaneously, while balancing myself in the heart. Seeking the light only is as foolish as trying to eliminate the southern hemisphere of our planet.

Over the following months, I regularly slow down and focus into my heart. I am still quite a way from the centre, where a fine balance between the spiritual and the human is possible.

I am aware of the various levels and functions of the heart. Blood comes in, is purified, and then sent out to the extremities of the body. It is an automatic process. There is no competition between the ventricles. Everything works together seamlessly and in complete harmony, if allowed to. It is no different on the psychic level. There is no need for protection then.

Maisie and I continue to visit historic churches with stuck energy. One of these, St Boltophs, has a paedophile past stretching back to the fifteenth century. This is serious ghost busting but the trapped spirits there are needing forgiveness not censure. We give it to them and the church is cleared.

֎

To become a much tougher healer, I must deal with some of my own issues that are still preventing me from addressing the deeper, darker karmas that lie behind the ill health in those who come to me.

I have started attracting clients who have taken the mind-expanding drug LSD, often years ago, which has left their psychic doorways vulnerable. They are now hearing voices, sometimes telling them to do precarious things. On speaking to these past entities, I learn that most of them are very angry because they had positions of power and authority on earth but, over in the spirit world, they have none.

I have just received an urgent call for help from Ivan, one of our clients, who has recently started to behave irrationally. When I arrive, it is not Ivan I am confronted by but a tyrannical Roman past life coming through him, who certainly does not want to listen to reason.

"How dare you try to prevent me regaining my power – you little person." was his first rant. "I could have you eliminated. Traitor to my name." Much more vicious threats follow thick and fast.

I try to get Ivan to slow down and focus himself, but he feels trapped and panics. Then, without warning, he dives out of the first-floor window to get away from this relentless attack. I can do nothing to stop him. The immense shock is compounded when it takes almost an hour, in a nearby phone box, to get the ambulance to attend to his broken leg jutting out.

"I cannot accept your assertion, sir, that the patient has given his permission for us to come. I need to speak to him in person."

Ivan survives but keeps away from me. Several weeks later, a phone call from his uncle lets me know that he had started believing that he was a Buddhist monk, with a responsibility to suffer for the sins of the world. Yesterday, he poured kerosene over his body and set fire to it.

A great deal of soul searching is needed. Will I continue with the spirit rescue work that Maisie is training me to do?

8

Achieving balance at last.

My life in London reverts to the very mundane and my efforts to find permanent premises for the healing work are not succeeding. Though Helios is now a charity, we are still dependent on licensed squats to house our work. Twice, after painting and decorating yet another house and having attracted in some interesting therapists, Camden Council throws us out again.

I wander the streets regularly looking for something permanent, closer to the centre of London, but the interesting prospects that Maisie encourages me to pursue, a flat above a car park in Marylebone, a deserted parsonage in Euston, come to nothing.

With so many friends falling ill and dying from AIDS, I become totally immersed in all that means for the many people involved with our work, infected and affected. Four of us start a weekly empowerment and healing group in the Friends Meeting House in St Martin's Lane. Surely, we can overcome this scourge using spiritually-based methods and focused healing energy.

It soon becomes clear that the karma underlying this condition is far too ingrained for us to succeed at this time. Our healing does, at least, bring respite and much comfort to the sick and the dying. While the promiscuity of many in the gay community is the main factor, I do need to understand the spiritual reason for this epidemic.

People only get ill when there is something out of balance and this, very often, stems from lives of barbarity and oppression far back. As I delve deeper, I can see that much of this particular karma is rooted in the beliefs and actions of the Roman Catholic Church. I am thinking of the Spanish inquisition, but that isn't it.

My mind then turns to the persecution of the Cathars in 13th century France. The Albigensian Crusade to eliminate heresy is estimated to have killed 1 million people and I can inwardly see that many of those contracting HIV at this time had past lives responsible for this.

The hypocrisy and sexual guilt promulgated by the churches over the centuries still lies deep within the souls of very many people alive today. HIV will remain with us until there is a genuine willingness to deal with this,

Our AIDS programmes using holistic therapy and mind training are not gaining any acceptance in orthodox circles. Indeed, I am being criticised regularly for recommending them and there are several attempts to close us down. Without any effective drugs, more of our clients are falling ill. It is to our credit that very few are dying. As the government is paying little attention, I become politically engaged and much angrier.

1989

The enlightenment intensives launched my spiritual journey and provided the impetus for all that followed but I have become weighed down by the boring administrative work attached to our healing work. Enlightenment should have taken me beyond all that, surely. Jeff Love had returned to America and his replacements were clearly not up to scratch. I hadn't given the process a thought for ages. Yesterday, I learnt that Jake Chapman, who had trained as an enlightenment master, is running them several times a year.

Could a relative beginner have enough deep understanding to go with me into the really daunting places that I will probably have to explore with him? I contact him anyway. He convinces me enough to attend his three-day November intensive in an atmospheric old manor house in Devon, with Mandeley mists and the moor not far away.

I position myself in front of my first partner and though I want to venture into fertile inner places, I have lost my fervour and don't quite know where to place my intention. In past intensives, prior to enlightenment, I always had a number of mental shifts, suddenly seeing that the opposite of my beliefs was actually true. But now, I am feeling the need to focus higher.

I speak first about my disappointments as a writer. I love the theatre and come alive when in rehearsal for shows, but as I work through the many rejections, I let out a cry, "I am waiting for the world to get its act together and (pause for effect) notice me."

At the end of the second day, the reverse revelation comes, "The world is waiting for me to get my act together." I bounce back defiantly with "Surely I have done enough," followed by a very sad realisation, that if I do become a successful writer, this will take me away from the spiritual work that I need to do. Am I ready for anonymity for the rest of my life? Not yet. "Let me have just a short period of recognition," I plead to my guardians, "and then I will."

This is enough for my fully determined self to return and, at the end of the three days, a breakthrough comes. Light is pouring down into me from above and "I am the Creator" bursts out. I report it to Jake and he says, rather casually, "Oh yes, that is the second level prior to enlightenment." I am not especially disappointed but it raises a raft of questions that I don't ask and one that I do. "When is your next Intensive?"

"I am holding a two-week one in the Summer next year," leads to an immediate, "Book me on it."

I have never found this process difficult. Some find the long stretches, where nothing much happens, hard to bear, particularly on the second day, often accompanied by nagging headaches and drowsiness. To get through the boredom, I remain still and present for long periods of time. I know the blocks will clear if I am patient but what would 14 days of this be like? Jake assures me that, after the third day, most people slip into a comfortable routine, accepting what comes.

1990

This intensive attracts 14 participants, mainly women, to Jake and Eva's house near Milton Keynes. Jake has an exceptional ability to stay present through the many hours of dyads. He never hands over to a monitor as Jeff Love did but, despite this, I am not feeling that he really understands me or is at all aware of the process I am going through. His descriptions of enlightenment seem very abstract and other worldly.

Doubts, such as, "Perhaps I had never been enlightened," flood in but I dismiss them. Jeff gave me his sign of approval.

The other participants are all well-meaning. That sounds like a judgement and probably is. They are playing their role of listener but little more. It was only when I am on one of my walks or during a working contemplation outside that I direct my desire for further enlightenment, into myself, with renewed fervour. I don't need anyone else then.

In the early dyads, I proceed on from the answer reached last time, "I am the creator". I had thought a lot about this during the intervening months. "Do I, as the Creator, exist within the physical reality, or outside it – or, more likely, both?" Of course, everything is God, so I cannot, in any of my manifestations and bodies, be separate from Him.

I am focusing into the crown chakra, gradually building up enough intensity there, looking for a way to break through into the realms beyond. Sometimes, it seems as though I will explode.

To be what I really am, my ego must accept its annihilation. But permanently? It has always returned post-enlightenment but, if I do reach the top of my body and break through into a much higher reality there, will my ego return then?

I inch upwards, close to the brink now, where surrender will be inevitable. It is still necessary to present anything that comes up to my current partner, the doubts especially. My ego seems to be ready to leap into the abyss, but the brink suddenly moves on and there are new obstacles in the way.

As the days progress, I report all my resistances to letting go. "Do I really want the responsibility of being even more enlightened than I already am?" That sounds smug, Greg. Stop it!

I want no barriers between my conscious and subconscious minds. The two must spontaneously blend into a common purpose but my partners are just not there for me at that level.

"Isn't there anyone out there who can become one with me?", I shout, earning Jake's obvious displeasure, but I continue, "My twin soul, where the hell are you?"

Surely the creator, that I am, can't do it alone. Why create anything if there is no one to share it with? One tree doesn't make a forest and one human being does not make a tribe. These superficial thoughts tumble around in my already overloaded skull.

It is the last day, and I am no longer directing my intention inwards at all, only further and further up. As I spiral towards the crown chakra, my mind tries to interfere but I must continue on. I desperately want to escape this reality.

I am reprimanded by some angelic being for having the temerity to want to be special in God's eyes. "Humility is crap," I shout. "Give me everything!"

I go over old ground. There is always a time lag, however minute, between the time my eyes register a scene and when the brain and the mind acknowledge it. There are stars we see in the sky that haven't actually been there for millennia. So, my sense awareness cannot ever be in the present moment.

The mind is unable to experience the absolute. Many people describe enlightenment, but that is just the subdued ego's interpretation after the event. Though the steady blissful state continues for a time, eventually, there is no holding the ego back.

Enlightenment is both nothing and everything, simultaneously, with the Zen task to find the middle way. At this point, I am making a very firm decision, to risk everything for that moment of total surrender.

Out on our final afternoon walk, I know that the bell will soon summon us dutifully back to the group room. I am not ready for that. Enlightenment must happen out in the open, right away from "those people". Rebellious thoughts are taking over and, with them, the final fears, "Total surrender? Christ, no! Anything but that!" Am I ready to be a simple holy man, meditating half the day, loving everyone but not being involved with any of them intimately. A sudden shift jolts me into, "Yes, I am!"

A vertical pillar of consciousness is now passing through my crown, straight down to my base chakra and on from there. I am being held within clear bounds that exclude any experience of the three-dimensional reality, which has now disappeared completely. I am approaching a state of pure detachment.

The breakthrough moment is looming but there is still one step to be taken. I must entirely let go of the earth. Up is the only way to go. I slam my focussed intention violently into the crown chakra again and again. I must break through. Another slam and suddenly, I shout, "There is only...." a 'ping.'

That was it. I am revolving in both directions simultaneously, entirely within the column. It seems that eternity and infinity, light and dark are making love within me in the here and now. Suddenly, I am shooting like an arrow, in slow motion, through the crown vortex and along a tunnel between worlds into another reality altogether.

I remain conscious and alert within the total darkness around me. I can just make out figures, maybe those who oversee everything, not guides or guardians, beyond them - the wise ones. I am detached, yet totally involved. I ask no questions of these radiant beings, yet understanding comes to me.

They are there and then they aren't, each a pulsating presence, coming and going. I am embracing being and non-being simultaneously. It is impossible to interpret what I am experiencing. Manifestation follows intention instantaneously. When I accept what is, knowing is automatic.

Then, one of the group of beings surrounding me is suddenly closer and more defined. I am used to this happening. We link up automatically. He says, "To fully participate in the divine creation, there are three important lessons. This is the first."

Everything he says resonates deeply and is profoundly understood. The heaviness of my life has been lifted and as long as I continue to focus into my heart, this amazing experience will keep going. It is similar to channelling, which requires total detachment so that the energy can be passed on uninterrupted.

This fabulous being seems to be standing on both sides of me. One aspect is emitting a brilliance that seems to be sucking part of me into a dark cavern within him, returning it from the other direction. A weird experience until I accept it fully. The more I want to make something happen or not happen, the more certainly I will fail.

To build up to the breakthrough moment, I had to accept both arms of the duality, that I am, simultaneously. Johosephat has shown me how to be anywhere at any time but now I am experiencing that far more completely. When I surrender to a genuine need inside of me, it is fulfilled. I am both a conduit and also an essential part of any manifestation. Without my involvement, nothing will work.

Another being, with feminine energy, is suddenly there, again on either side but behind me. I experience an upheaval of conflicted feelings, causing me to focus no longer into my heart but straight up. They retreat immediately.

"Will you never learn, Greg?", I chide.

Back in balance now, the dark opens out to reveal amazing formations and colour patterns that change constantly. An intense light makes many emotionally charged appearances through this. Everything seems infinite in its simple inter-related complexity. I am opening up to every revelation, trusting that it is what I need.

Of course, I could opt to stay here and explore further but I need to return to the field. How do I do that? I send out an ask to the now retreating figures but they keep on going. On instinctively returning to a heart-orientated balance, the "I" re-positions itself down my central column. I instinctively add the "am" – two letters representing duality. That is enough and I start my descent back to the waiting three- dimensional human reality.

It is like going down in a lift, stopping briefly at each floor and a different time, to be confronted by the life I'd led then. I recognise some of them, but they don't remain there long enough to make contact. One after the other, and then the last few, the French woman, the Belgian followed by the Australian and the Indian man, before I touch down on terra firma with a mighty jolt.

Immediately after, the bell summons us to the final session. I don't feel connected to the others in the room at all. They are on their own personal journeys, so I report nothing to them about what has happened. Afterwards, they tell me that I am glowing. I only just manage to voice a single goodbye.

I hurry to Jake to tell him of my experience, but he says that it is over and he is too tired to receive any further input. A surge of anger rises up. I flash back to my time in the womb when my mother had been in a state of hating her father for the rejections he had inflicted on her. She was blind in one eye as a result for most of those nine months. Both are forgiven.

Even though this breakthrough is indelibly etched on my soul and cannot be denied, I am feeling terribly vulnerable now. I know that this major turning point in my life is not the end of the journey. There are still many more experiences to come before I will remain unaffected by the world.

The following Thursday, I enthusiastically visit Maisie to tell her all about my experiences. "Well", she begins, initially reluctant to look me in the eyes but, on doing so, immediately switches into her full 'sussing out what's going on behind the scenes' mode. "Well, you did half what you went there for."

What!?", I would normally have responded, "I went out through the crown chakra into this other dimension, awarely. How many people you know have done that? Half?!!!" - but I didn't. In a sudden, painful to accept moment, I realise that I now have to burst through the base chakra post-enlightenment, and go equally as far down into the earth where, I sense, there are many dangers waiting for me.

Johosephat comes near and assures me that if I remain in the heart nothing can affect me down there. Maisie teaches a protection method, but I am not sure that I need it now.

"Most people need help to keep the nasty energies out," she insists and then explains her process in some detail, based on the five-pointed star, which ends with, "I place myself under the protection of Almighty God and his Son, Jesus the Christ.

"Oh Maisie," I protest, "haven't you anything without Him in it?" She changes it to "I place myself under the protection of the Divine Presence and all those who come from the spheres of light."

"Maisie. I'm a dark worker!"

"Then, this isn't for you," she snaps back, not fully understanding what I am saying,

"Most people are not in their hearts, Maisie. They reach up mentally to the Father for His support." My own father, who has recently disinherited me, flashes into my mind. "Where is the Divine Mother in all of this?"

She finishes off with, "True. There is nothing to be frightened of when you come into balance."

ಇ

Since first marching against the Vietnam war, I have gone on many rallies holding up provocative banners rubbishing our leaders' many attempts to undermine our traditional rights or condemning them for riding roughshod over the needs of the marginalised - but I have never wanted to be a front line activist. I am reluctant to visit the women's peace camp at Greenham Common, feeling that I must now find another way to make a difference.

I am immensely pleased when Maisie starts her Peacemakers' Guild to bring light and upliftment into situations of global unrest. Each circle member links up with a specific leader who needs to change to a more inclusive mindset, detailing how this can be achieved. I concentrate on those denying the AIDS crisis, Thatcher, Reagan and their ilk.

With Maisie, I have often focused into the hearts of difficult dead people who are encouraging those leaders to do reprehensible things, while also confronting the ones in the background who influence them. There are always plenty to choose from but, now, we are concentrating on morally dead live people.

We tackle the Tiananmen Square massacre. I am particularly concerned about this, as is a past Chinese life of mine. I spend many hours focussing healing into that situation. As soon as it has settled down there, I am on the first plane from London allowed into Beijing, determined to find out first-hand what had happened but, once there, no one will talk to me about it.

Although it is very early days for this kind of spiritual work, I like to think that we are getting some Presidents and Prime Ministers to change direction, even a dictator or two. I am honing the skills needed to work effectively with those on the subtle levels able to influence the many British politicians and their advisers who are going seriously astray. I regularly stand outside the Downing Street gates sending heart energy into the cabinet room, during their meetings, while grounding myself and, hopefully, one or two of them.

My ideas and abilities are further developed on a New York trip where I am invited to participate in a workshop run by two Indian men who had been trained to carry forward Gandhi's unifying work after his assassination. They did not succeed because those behind partition harboured motives based in religious intolerance who could not be less in the Gandhian mould.

I've always been drawn to the Mahatma and his determination to see the British Raj leave India. This workshop revealed exactly why the principles and procedures he used in his work have been so little understood and practised since. I am determined to adapt them to my political work. On returning to London, I hurry to Maisie's house, demanding to speak to him.

During Gandhi's early time in London as a student at the Inner Temple, one of the city's four law colleges, he observed the establishment people that he met and studied under. He also unlocked a tremendous affinity with this country and its people, and had a deep wish that it would, one day, become truly great. He knew that this would not happen while they controlled an empire.

"I can feel myself to be both Indian and English. There is almost a love affair between the two countries within me because of the strong influence from my former lives in both countries that were influencing me."

"I have a deep understanding of how true personal power is generated and the balances that must be put into place before the methods I am developing can work. My first principle is the most difficult to implement - expressed in the second commandment of Jesus, "Love thy neighbour as thyself" coupled with His, "Forgive them, Lord, for they know not what they do", when on the cross. Loving the English was certainly a pre-requisite for addressing the repressive control of the British Raj."

The Indian system still relies on the English penchant for a small elite to control the masses. The class/caste systems were based on a centuries-old belief, that they had a God-given right to rule. Both countries were forced to absorb many other groups and faiths, however. India had its Buddhists, Muslims, Jains and Sikhs while England needed to assimilate the Saxons, Celts, Romans, Vikings and Normans. The karmic elements left over from these intrusions have never been well worked out.

"I was appalled when seeing the discrimination experienced as an Indian immigrant in South Africa and how the ruling elite controlled the justice system. If they didn't want you to win, you had no chance. So, a more effective way was needed that did not engage the British where they were strong."

The turning point came on a train journey to Pretoria when Gandhi was thrown out of a first-class railway compartment and beaten up, after refusing to give up his seat to a European passenger. He began developing and teaching the principles of satyagraha - truth, compassion and firmness – often wrongly interpreted as a passive resistance to authority.

"I now know that it is essential to be very firm, even forceful, when standing up to oppressors."

Gandhi developed as an occultist, as I am doing. He directed heart energies precisely into serious situations and resistant people, hoping for a lasting transformation.

When occultists venture into the public arena, they are usually feared. They are at the adept stage of development - trainee masters who need to prove themselves in the public arena and some are assassinated.

Gandhi was very psychically attuned but, within the Indian tradition, he had to pose as a humble holy man, which was definitely not his true nature. When asked if he was a mystic trying to be a politician, he replied that "No, I am a politician trying to be a mystic."

He saw that the English elite work from the throat chakra. They ruled the empire by the force of their self-belief, at that level of authority, which easily kept them above the more earth-orientated locals they wished to subjugate. "Carry my bags, would you? There's a good chap."

However, this was unbalanced and when Gandhi came along, being heartless, they were vulnerable to the loving energies he directed into the empty spaces where compassion should be.

"I learnt to harness my anger by focussing it into my own heart where it built up and became a tremendous force. I taught this to my small group of devoted followers, with the overwhelming support of the Indian people. Then, I stepped forward to direct this power gently but precisely into their hollow hearts. The Raj ran amok for awhile, killing some of the protesters, but we eventually sent them packing."

I thank the great man and when Maisie comes out of trance, she announces, "Gandhi was the angriest man on the planet." This is hard to accept when considering the image he portrayed but it could well have been true.

I add this understanding to everything I've learnt over the years to deal with those souls on the spirit side who are still seeking power over others. They usually come through Maisie, convinced that they will win easily. I have gradually simplified my practices into a clear four-stage process based on the simple model of the three-dimensional equidistant cross. The three arms intersect in the heart. The dynamism within the personal sphere around me, feeds and motivates all of the earth energy and spirit release work that I do.

Energetically, it is three double helixes meeting in the heart: the vertical Father/ Mother one, the masculine/ feminine duo out to the sides with the future, straight ahead, balancing the past, lying an equal distance behind.

The yang impulse is focussed precisely into the heart and, from this point of balance, the yin element is automatically liberated, expanding out along the three arms to entirely fill my personal energy sphere. The yin and yang components are then drawn into a unified working whole.

I breathe in fully, pausing before breathing out very slowly through the nose in a series of stages, until there is no air left at all in the lungs. At the same time, the fore and middle fingers, of both hands, have gradually come round to the heart, and a precisely balanced power is directed into a deep place within it. This is the essential key to accessing my full inner potential. Then the fore and middle fingers of my left hand shoot up towards my highest potential in the sky, with two fingers of the right hand likewise pointing far down into the earth. I breathe in again, firming up the central pillar, my true 'I'.

With my masculine embracing the feminine and my future embracing the past, there is a lot of spontaneous release happening. I am very aware of my never quiet ego, on the sidelines, doing its best to divert my efforts

I follow this with a few normal breaths before repeating the slow full-breath routine. This may seem simple in theory but it is surprising how often people resist doing at least one part of the exercise, usually the extended out-breath, which prevents it from working fully.

The final step is to allow any resistances to vibrate up the central pillar from the earth, also through the feet. With the physical resistances released, I allow spontaneous yawning, shaking and coughing followed by laughter, tears and righteous anger to release the emotional blocks in stages. All of this is underpinned by fear which is then fully expressed through the body vibrations that complete the process.

By going precisely straight down into the earth via the base chakra, while contained within the central pillar, my body is effectively freed up as those polarised energies come up to create a fully liberated vibration, with the deepest karma being relieved.

This simple procedure, requiring a very precise heart focus, is an exceptionally powerful way to remove personal karma and to develop psychic sensitivity.

I attract no opposing forces or negative entities, though they will always try to lure me back into the mind where they can interfere. Achieving balance is essential for any work involving malevolent spirits.

I am focussing now at the intersection point in the depths of my heart to achieve a fully integrated reality. There are a number of disruptive past lives around me, trying to attract my attention. Scenes of Egypt are coming up and I know that I must go there, followed by other linked places. Rome and Paris come to mind. I must be much more adventurous now.

However, keeping the healing initiative going and developing our response to the AIDS crisis, is leaving me little time to embark on this many times postponed Egyptian trip. In any case, I am not sure I would enjoy it. Friends, who went there, reported that they were besieged by countless local lads trying to part them from their money with promises of pleasure at bargain prices that didn't materialise. And there is the notorious tummy bug.

It is much more important to find and establish suitable premises for our holistic therapy services to the many seriously ill people coming to us for treatment.

The eureka moment comes in November 1991 when I come across the perfect place, a run-down Greater London Council building in a Kings Cross back street. It is still a sleazy area, so the rent is affordable. We have savings enough to survive for well over a year and HIV funding should be easy to secure to keep it going beyond that. Maisie gives her "go ahead", and I boldly make a down payment on half of the first floor.

At a hastily called trustees' meeting, we change the charity's name to reflect our step forward. We want to be seen as dispensing wisdom and healing from on high, so we choose Akhenaten's Sun God as our inspiration, but neither the "Ra Centre" or the "Aten Community" appeal to us. We switch to Greek mythology and, the following April, we open our doors as "The Helios Centre."

It is an exciting time. Finding enough committed therapists is the easy part. Funding is much more elusive. A natural therapy centre nearby receives grants but they are the only ones the statutory funders are willing to support. Two years later, we have run out of money and failure is fast closing in. But no, wait on, the partner of one of our clients is the drummer for the pop star, George Michael. She asks George to be our saviour and, in due course, he arrives on his white charger, with just enough money to keep us going.

9
Our Egyptian Adventure
1995

Helios has become a vibrant community with seventeen therapists and a full book of clients. Akhenaten continues to give illuminating talks through Maisie and, one afternoon, when taking questions about his life in Egypt, he firmly asks me, "When are you going to Thebes? It is long overdue."

I respond, "Later this year," but realise, soon after, that I don't want to travel alone. This is resolved when an unexpected email arrives from Martin, a pianist and composer I met in New York, "Have you gotten around to visiting Luxor yet?" He's been before but his inner promptings are demanding a return. We agree that we must avoid the tourist parties and venture into the real Egypt in search of its hidden history.

I book us into the Emilio, a shabby but rather pleasant 2* hotel, where they advise us to set out at sunrise because, in September, it is unbearably hot by mid-day. We start with the usual sites, the tombs and temples on the West bank, but when we get to Karnak Temple, on the third day, I sense that it is about to get serious.

As Martin and I begin walking down the central aisle of that impressively pillared temple, I spontaneously reach out to hold his hand. It comes to me that we were married in Thebes and I was the wife. Everyone we pass appears to be from those times. I glance across to my husband and feel sudden, severe apprehension. We reach the end and my wobbly legs are telling me to sit down. I ask spirit to fill me in.

The communicator is my spirit friend Johosephat, "It was the time of Ramses the Second and Martin was Pthatuk, a very ambitious member of the minor nobility."

Out with the guidebook and the list of Pharaohs, down to Tutankhamun, Seti, Ramses I & then II, who is better known as Ramses the Great. He certainly lived up to his exalted title by completely wiping out any last vestiges of the Akhenaten reforms before re-conquering much of the territory lost by that 'weak heretic pharaoh'.

Small in stature but great in other ways. Over a very long life, his many wives presented him with around 50 sons, and more than 40 daughters, which made his succession fairly secure. How did he find time to fight all those wars?

Further meditation confirms that neither Martin's past life nor mine had approved of his conquests - on the battlefields, that is. Another question arises: Why did our former lives marry when both of us are yang by nature, innately attracted to feminine partners? This is unanswered until we return to the temple, on the following evening, for a 'sound and light show' which gives us the chance to wander around the monuments unsupervised.

I locate the statue of Ramses II and sit contemplating beneath it. The story unfolds: Maisie's former life was a silly, giggly emotional nonentity unable to command the home or discipline the servants – temperamentally opposite to her previous Queen Ty persona. Everyone expected her to marry Pthatuk but he wanted a more assertive wife to support his quest for influence in the court. He needed the authority to bring about the much-needed reforms to this hierarchical system.

So, he chose my former life, Amisi, a forceful yang woman, who was a sister to Maisie's life then, and equally determined to see Ramses overthrown, so that Egypt would be a more considerate neighbour to the civilisations it was cruelly subjugating.

Pthatuk and Amisi were a formidable team, and

they rose up the social ladder, fawning at the feet of the Pharaoh while plotting to undermine his authority behind the scenes. In doing so, they influenced many people to support them. But Pthatuk was not a subtle character, and not nearly discreet enough in his planning. Ramses found out and the couple was seized by the palace guards. Without any kind of trial of public humiliation, they were secretly sedated and placed into coffins - then buried alive.

The next morning, Martin and I are strolling the Nile bank on the way to hire a felucca, one of the small traditional sailing boats, to take us up river. A young man approaches who enthusiastically says, in disjointed bursts of English, that a friend, Amad, the skipper of one of these ancient crafts, will take us wherever we want to go. I refrain from my usual, "Go away, kid. We don't need your help." I am seduced by his enormous smile and can do nothing but follow.

Once on board, we learn that we have been picked up by Barakat, a sixteen-year-old village lad who has only just reached the age when he can use the family mini-bus to ferry tourists around in. He is very shy but I know that his flashing eyes will win me over every time.

Further up the river, Amad suggests we remove our clothes to take in the sun, which we do, almost without thinking. He obligingly rubs sun cream all over us. I close my eyes, breathe a sigh of contentment and start to imagine, in lurid detail, that I am a sheik.

Barakat isn't participating in this ritual but sits cross-legged taking it all in. When he does want to say things to us, and that is often, Amad interprets. We are determined to locate the hidden Luxor and, for this, Barakat enthusiastically volunteers to become our guide for the rest of the trip.

That evening, he drives us to a special cabaret recommended by his cousin in a former down-market hotel. We are stopped at the door by a couple of hoodies lurking outside but when Barakat gives his cousin's name, they welcome us in. He has totally misunderstood the nature of our relationship for all of the tourists present are same-sex couples.

The female attendant showing us to our table is obviously a man. Later, 'she' is the first act, letting out a haunting rendition of anguished love, the kind that Egyptian divas love to sing. Rather good, actually. 'She' is followed by an extremely lascivious belly dancer who drops trinkets onto her midriff, aiming them accurately at members of the audience. The women are cheering her on. The men manage a smirk.

Then the M.C. asks for a couple from the audience to come forward and perform a dance. No one offers until, suddenly, Barakat yanks me onto the stage with him. He is clearly the stud and I am the seducible fem. Fortunately, from my early career as an actor specialising in comedy roles, I know how to carry it off.

Demure now, I look at him warily from around a raised hand, reluctant to succumb to his enticements, a bit fluttery. He takes a step forward. I respond with several rapid hops backwards, cocking my head to one side and discreetly moving my hips in sync with the music. I evade every subsequent attempt to take hold of me, with large unexpected side steps. It is great fun, and we are applauded enthusiastically at the end.

We return to our table and glasses of bubbly are provided. Barakat declines his, not, as I later discover, because he doesn't drink. There are various dives around town, that the authorities turn a blind eye to, where tourists can buy locals a beer. But here, in a more formal setting, as a Moslem, he isn't allowed to touch the sinful stuff. We accept the cheap fizz, though we didn't order it, and a bill is placed in front of us.

We have left our money at the hotel and Barakat is skint, as well. So, we make a cautious withdrawal, smile at the lookouts outside and then scamper up the alley, faster when the proprietor appears at the door shouting at his guards to pursue us. Fortunately, we reach the busy main road, with police around, and slip away uncaught.

As promised, Barakat arrives very early at the hotel the following morning and takes us across to the West Bank to watch the sun rise over Luxor. He sits beside us, fascinated by our contemplative approach to the environment. I also discover that he is a natural healer when he places his hands on my shoulders.

We are suffering from tomb overload, so Barakat takes us to a Coptic Monastery some distance into the desert, looked after by nuns. It is Sunday and, as we arrive, a priest is inviting all the men into his service. The women and children are relegated to an adjacent room, able to hear the proceedings but not participate.

As Barakat speaks little English, he isn't able to give us any information about the sites we visit but, as he is so cheerfully willing, I forgive him everything, even when he drops and chips one of the statues I've bought after a hard bartering session at the bazaar.

On the sixth day, he takes us to meet his aunt in a nearby village. Being with the locals, in their home environment, is the most enjoyable and rewarding part of the trip. We can now better understand their casual subservience to the rituals of their religion and the chauvinistic way they order their society.

Very few tourists go anywhere near the villages. The women are scared of the Egyptian men, with some justification. They treat their wives and their animals very roughly. I have to stop Barakat kicking a donkey when it won't get out of his way. We also witness an incident in the main street when a horse and cart man accidentally clips a police car. They beat him almost to a pulp in front of us.

In the village, the women come into their own. His aunt's family includes a deformed girl who is far better looked after than she would be in our society. The male and female worlds only come together at mealtimes. Enormous platters are conjured up from tiny, poorly appointed kitchens with a large variety of delicious helpings to choose from.

Barakat promised to drive us to the airport on the morning of our departure, but he hasn't shown up. I have to accept that this has been a holiday encounter and I will not see him again. This pains me because I feel he would be a very good link for the earth energy work I'll have to do on my next visit to Luxor.

Back in London, I waste no time in arranging a second trip for the following March. Jill, who was a member of my early development circle, and Andrew, the centre osteopath, enthusiastically agree to accompany me.

Looking down as we circle Luxor airport, I tune into deeper resonances of that city. A warm familiar glow spreads over me, followed by tears as we land. I have never really felt at home in London, but Luxor is a special place for me. As we step out from the customs checks, Barakat is there in front of us, touting for business. Amazing synchronicity. He agrees to pick us up at our hotel early the next morning.

When we explore the tombs, I pretend to be an expert tour guide rather well. It only takes a few discreet glances at the guidebook before each site to keep up the pretence. I accidentally take them into a neglected underground tomb without any wall paintings or lighting. Shining the torch upwards, we disturb a hanging array of bats.

"Do they suck blood?", Jill whispers.

"Yes," we cheekily affirm. Her subsequent scream causes them to flap around us making things much worse.

Back in Luxor, I continue my search for Akhenaten. I had assumed that none of his relics were left after the complete purge by his successors, but the wall paintings in the tomb of his Grand Vizier, Ramose, are still largely intact.

There is also a small temple at Karnak, stripped of any obvious connection to Akhenaten but, after focussed contemplation, I am getting a clear impression of how it was in its glory days. This 'Temple of Amenhotep IV', his official title, was constructed outside the boundaries of the Precinct of Amon-Re, to the east. The main temple in the complex was named Gempaaten, which means "The Sun Disc is found in the Province of the God Aten".

It is a neglected and forlorn site but I am aware that it is still connected to an inner temple that the spirit of Akhenaten inhabits when he wishes to assist with working out the Egyptian karma. On sitting to meditate, I can feel him joining me, eager to pass on further information.

It is easy to view Akhenaten's life as a failure. He came to power at a high point in the glory times of Egypt. The long journey into the shadows escalated when his father Amenhotep III, the ninth pharaoh of the 18th Dynasty, (Maisie's husband in this life) came to the throne. He had been a great warrior and was not backward in cruelly inflicting his country's might onto the surrounding civilisations.

To instil the principles of soldiery, his young son was twice taken to where captured enemies were held and he was forced to watch them being killed.

"I was appalled at the brutality of it," he tells me. "I wanted to bow down only to the God of love which is why I chose Ra, the Sun God, as my ideal."

"When the time came for the mantle of Pharaoh to fall upon me, I knew that the Priesthood was corrupt. They took bribes when testifying in the Hall of Judgment and insisted on generous payments to give wealthy citizens special access to a particular god."

The generals still sent troops, into far places, seeking out prosperous communities they might profitably overwhelm and subjugate. It didn't take much to start a battle that they were sure to win. He had seen Syria conquered for the riches that came as spoils of war and many slaves were taken. This, Akhenaten abhorred.

He was determined to rid Thebes of corruption and vice. Naturally, this was resisted by the power elite.

"I was very young then and did not know how to implement the ideals that were glowing golden in my heart and mind. I wanted to surround myself with creative people and wise spiritual teachers. As a boy, I loved spending time with the ones who tilled the ground, who showed me that the worlds beneath the earth were not as tradition held them to be."

When the sight was clear and the emotions less troubled, Akhenaten was able to see into the hearts of those who came for judgement and only once condemned the wrong man. He stopped the practice of forfeiting lives. Many times, he wrestled with these moral dilemmas as he developed the noble ideals that came to him in his quiet times. These were sometimes too large for his mind to encompass and they had a habit of vanishing as soon as they appeared.

After several stressful years of trying to get the Priests of Amun to give up their unscrupulous practices and the military to restrain their urge for further conquests, Akhenaten reluctantly concluded that this would not happen. There were too many foes, too many ready to twist his decisions and call his ideas a farrago of nonsense. He did not condemn them. They had to grow into understanding in their own time.

He tried to convince some senior priests to join his cause but few accepted. He would also need military protection, when so far from Thebes. So, he sent his close advisors out to recruit volunteers. There was one free-thinking general that they confidently expected would support the pacifist ideals. They talked to him often about this, but the man could not take the step. Akhenaten then told me that this was a former life of mine. He then approached younger men who gladly took up the chance of promotion.

So, Akhenaten and his court, sailed down the Nile to found the city of Amarna. There, a fresh outpouring of creative energy would come into being, with new architecture and a more humane social system, where life would be inspired by the Aten. I can hear the marvellous hymn that started and ended their day, still being sung by choirs in the ethers.

*"Wondrous you appear on the horizon,
Oh, living Aten, source of all life,
Rising triumphant in the eastern heavens,
Filling the land with your radiant love."*

All of the Amarna art was realistic, not the flat perspective commissioned by other Pharaohs. Akhenaten wanted his family pictures to be natural so that they were fully alive and inspiring to the viewer.

Everyone in the city received the teaching and training suited to their lives and talents. The peasantry was taught that they had an immortal soul and that the Aten would welcome them into the afterlife regardless of whether their relatives, left behind, could pay for the privilege or not. They were taught to cultivate an inner source of being and a willingness to put aside self-interest for the good of the whole community. Even many who were illiterate had access to wise men, especially chosen by the pharaoh, to arouse understanding in the chambers of their minds that would enlighten the path for them.

I can fully appreciate the vast splendour of the city of Aton which, though completely destroyed, still lives on in the world of spirit, built now of energy, not stone. Why was the dream not realised so that people would come from far places to experience the creative joys of that beautiful city, to feel the new vibrations, hear the new strains of music, see the beautiful works of art and to sit at the feet of those who taught monotheism? Well, of course, it was not the right time for it to succeed.

Akhenaten then tells me that my former life had thought more deeply about his decision to not accompany him to Amarna.

"This is why I came to the earth" he realised, "to serve my Pharaoh." But there were problems to overcome. He couldn't resign his post and desertion was again a capital crime. The military was now completely controlled by the Theban elite. Nevertheless, he left his family behind and found an excuse to travel close to Amarna where he defected. He was determined to support Akhenaten and his vision, but he was too late to be of much use.

Nefertiti had felt the oncoming danger and left the city, taking her children with her. She could not muster the courage to stand beside her husband through it. Akhenaten, with his heart unsupported, could no longer sustain the determination needed for his important initiative. The presence of soldiers there had previously deterred any attack but it became known that he would not order them to take up arms and fight.

Akhenaten knew that his venture could not continue and he sent most of his court away. A great agony gripped him as the city of Aton was being overrun and conquered. He believed, that the Aten had forsaken him.

Of course, this was untrue. Men come, in their time, to pave the way, to set a stream of evolutionary thought into motion and establish structures that have a great life potential within them, even though the full glory cannot take root at that time. Such was the City of Aton.

As Akhenaten, Lord of the Horizon, was passing broken-hearted into the spirit world, there appeared before him a figure that he had seen twice before as a shadowy image backed by the glorious Aten. He realised then that this was the coming Son of God who, endowed with the Christ consciousness, would transform the man Jesus into the exalted Son of the Sun.

He knew that behind the sun that gives life to all, another sun is there, and another behind that, for the light comes from the Godhead. He saw that, in proclaiming the one God, he was indeed the forerunner of Jesus who took it a step further by directing that light deep into the earth so that some of His power and might and glory could be shared with the Earth Mother.

Despite the great illness that seized his mortal frame, the Son of Peace saw the room filled with scenes of transcendent beauty that conquered all doubt. His mission had been fulfilled. It was in that moment of great realisation that the soul of Akhenaten left the earth.

Yes, it wasn't a failure, any more than Jesus going to the cross was a failure. After this kind of apparent defeat, something of lasting benefit builds up in the ethers of the earth which speaks the message loud and clear to those, in later times, who will carry the mission forward. It may still be quite a long way off, but when an impulse to chase a vision is felt and followed, the destination will most certainly be reached.

The young today are seeking for somewhere to put their faith but, while not entombed in the traditions of the past, most are not grounding it sufficiently for the Earth Goddess to speak directly to them. That was the lesson Akhenaten himself did not engage with. His experiment was to reform an elite society. It would have been impossible then for him to believe that those at the bottom had equal value but it was a step forward nonetheless.

The Priests of Amun still flourish in our halls of power today through their later incarnations. Quite a few current English politicians still retain their previous arrogant Egyptian attitude to the masses. Akhenaten is stressing that I must never give up on my quest to reveal the truth to them that the time is up for the material gods they have worshipped for so long. Their statues are breaking and a new way is beginning to emerge.

In those far-off days, if they had made a little more effort to break through the strongholds of the priesthood, history may have unfolded quite differently. Dreams are all very well, but they need to be set into motion through effort, through striving and, sometimes, through suffering. Humans are feeling animals, whose senses can never be heightened and quickened by indulging in what only brings happiness. We are also thinking beings needing to make good thought structures that the will can breathe life into.

I have kept the Helios Centre small because I know that this is the age of the compact group. The old temples, churches, and so forth, have had their day. And even as like attracts like in the spirit world, like attracts like here on Earth. We must communicate freely, in whatever group we are drawn to, while always respecting each other's point of view.

Truth often hides in words that we reject at first hearing. The great, many-faceted diamond of truth can register on many levels simultaneously. Just as the glorious Aten sent its many shining rays out to Egypt, I am aware that something of the glory of Thebes is casting its rays into the Egyptian hearts of those incarnate today who are wearing another coat of skin.

They are poor, many of them, when they were the elite in that former life, and the few who supported Akhenaten are registering, perhaps only dimly, that their efforts were not in vain when the vision, they shared with their Pharaoh, was cast aside.

Something is beginning to lighten their hearts. "Walk in it", their inner voices are saying. "Be not afraid, for that dim, shadowy figure, the glorious Son of Light that Akhenaten saw on his death bed, is surely the Son of the Sons of the Godhead, and will be so for all eternity."

On our visits, we visit many Luxor families gathered together at mealtime and speak of these things but their will to change is weak. Most are caught up in their religion and the need to eke out a living. They seem to accept what I present to them, but they know they can't do it alone, not just one family, nor even one village. The intention and the resolve must come from the entire community.

Life on earth today is hard and, even in the most worthwhile group initiatives, there is a weaning out of those who cannot withstand the challenges. The purpose of any spiritual group must always be to tend, clear and cleanse their little portion of the vineyard of God, just as the arising of the city of Aton, cleared and cleansed Egypt of some of its imperial karma.

It is now the small groups, here and there, that are setting up a conduit for the light to stream into places where the right kind of power needs to be cultivated, places where the son of man and the Son of God can visit and feel at home.

I am understanding now that those gifts of the past, lost because of the misuse of power in Egypt, can only return enhanced once the makers and the workers of mischief on this earth can no longer gain their power by taking it from others.

Many see themselves as light workers, but I am certainly developing as a dark worker, to be an inspiration to those still walking blindly through life, ignoring either the light or the dark, and entirely missing the beauty in the blending of both.

The third trip to Luxor is set for later that year with my friend, Gary, and our homoeopath, Anne, in tow. Barakat is now our full-time guide and although I have to go through the usual tomb visiting ritual, we are more interested in spending time with the folk in his village, learning how they approach their god, Allah, and how this dominates their village life.

Though his extended family owns a many-acred farm, with livestock and sugar cane fields, they live a frugal existence which is very happy, most of the time, with occasional chauvinist interludes.

We still have difficulty getting Barakat's mother to take the veil away from her face in the house when we are there, so that we can get to know her better. We see how the creative lives of some of the other wives, shackled to the domestic chores, are being stunted. The women gain their fulfilment away from the men. We get to know two of the female schoolteachers in the village very well. They have less restraints placed on them and are loved by everyone. "Come tomorrow," they insist. "There's a big event on."

A female Sufi master is visiting the village. Everyone turns out to welcome her. She waves from her car as it moves slowly around the sports field. The children throw posies into the vehicle while the village choir sings. I can feel something very profound happening. Barakat stays with us, waving non-stop. "I am Sufi", he says proudly. Beyond the joyfulness of the proceedings, I can see how liberated Egypt and other Moslem countries will become when they fully accept the female divinity, no longer tainted by the dominant male gene.

On the following trip, Barakat takes me to his new teacher, a Sufi monk who lives in a small hut in the desert near Luxor. He is sitting on his prayer mat playing a drum and flute. A woman devotee takes food to him twice a day and she is just leaving as we arrive. He speaks no English and gestures for me to meditate beside him. Although he seems to like me, I later learn that he warned Barakat not to get too close to me, fearing that my Western ways would corrupt him. Of course, he is right.

Further investigation reveals that my first Egyptian life provided slaves for the rich at the time of the 18th dynasty pharaoh Thutmose II. He had wanted to be part of the elite but needed to remain on the periphery, observing how power is used for both good and ill.

2002

The, grassroots supporting, Greater London Council, a truly effective socialist experiment, has been spitefully disbanded by Prime Minister Thatcher. The building that houses Helios is sold to a profit-driven firm, who will only renew the lease at double the rent. After moving to temporary accommodation, secure premises are eventually found in a much more respectable Kings Cross location, at less rent. Our new Jersey-based landlords are happy to rely on the rapidly rising property prices in the area to give them their tidy profit.

The new HIV drugs are ensuring that the physical health of most of our clients remains stable, and a few are starting to look at their deeper psychological issues. We widen our brief to serve people with a full range of immune system conditions and a really productive time for the charity is secured.

Maisie's 'Peacemakers Guild' is taking on more challenging behind-the-scenes work in the political field. The duplicitous Tony Blair is in power. It is easy to see that he is gradually positioning his party far away from its true grassroots nature which will only widen the social and financial inequalities that are dividing this country.

10

The final visits to Egypt

2003

While meditating in Karnak Temple, my interest switches away from the Pharaohs to the priesthood whose sole responsibility was to care for the gods and goddesses there.

The high priests are chosen by the Pharaoh, the supreme priest of Egypt, who maintains a clear link between the people and their gods. The religious consistency and traditions of the priesthood played a vital role but, by the time of Akhenaten, they have amassed wealth and power by selling access to particular deities, especially Amun, the 'King of the Gods', which now exceeds that of the Pharaoh.

The mystically-inclined Akhenaten is certainly not as politically inept as often depicted. He recognizes the danger of the cult of Amun becoming too powerful and is trying to prevent this through his reforms of the priesthood, by demoting all of the gods, except Ra, and bringing in monotheism.

Faced with over 2,000 years of religious tradition, his efforts are in vain. On the purely practical level, too many people owe their livelihood to the temple and the worship of the gods. Akhenaten's religious reforms were more a political manoeuvre by his advisors to undercut the power of the priesthood, than a sincere effort to end the corruption.

Later, the young Tutankhamun (c. 1336-1327 BC), abolishes his father's religion and the old ways quickly return. This was completed by Horemheb, who erased Akhenaten's name from history in outrage at his impiety. As usual, I have taken my group to the Valley of the Kings and, in the simple and largely deserted tomb of Horemheb, an inner voice tells me that it was during his reign that I had my third Egyptian life.

༄

By delving into the spiritual nature of the old traditions, I hope to complete the full line of my Egyptian development. The following day, as I sit quietly in the Karnak ruins seeking to stimulate further memories, I become aware of my former life in the Theban priesthood.

He tells me that his name is Sempeth and he seems to be a bit more intellectually precise than I am, though lacking my sense of humour. On entering the priesthood at an early age, he becomes part of the group responsible for the implementation of the spells that promise eternal life to the deceased.

While the educated Egyptian people of that time are normally too sophisticated to be caught up in the superstitions too much, when crises come, even they fear that evil spirits are attacking them, and are the first to bring offerings to the temple hoping their prayers will be answered. Sempeth is well aware that this is mumbo jumbo and not real magic.

However, there is a small group of especially gifted sem priests who still have some of the true abilities and secretly look after the deeper aspects of the traditional magic and seership. One is Johosephat who has been watching Sempeth's development for some time and he has chosen this moment to approach, offering to be his teacher and mentor. The young man leaps at the chance.

Johosephat had been there during the time of Akhenaten and worshipped the Aten. Initiations were still carried out in the great pyramid for the nobility and those involved in public service. It was part of their training as members of the ruling class but he saw, very clearly, how the pharaonic excesses had largely replaced the genuine traditions. He eventually gave up trying to influence the secular hierarchy onto a more balanced path.

Groups of up to a hundred would travel to the pyramid to receive conveyor belt initiations. Unfortunately, many of the priests of the pyramid had become very unbalanced and, in their hands, the initiations were no longer for strengthening the initiate's structure of spiritual capability. They were more a power thing than a truly compassionate wisdom practice.

Sempeth's journey there played a very significant part in the calendar, with a festival at the end. Each of his select band of companions was specially chosen to receive more private attention than most. Initiates are asked to choose a favourite god, representing oneness, to protect them, but they tend to choose the one they believe has the greatest power, usually Amun-Ra, who is back in favour after his demotion by Akhenaten.

Johosephat is still in touch with a priest friend from earlier days, Karlesh, who was born into the ancient tribe of nomadic people with a heritage reaching back to the Atlantean times. He carries out an especially balanced initiation.

Sempeth is attracted to the Set god, which has a quite ambivalent presence. When balanced, it is a powerful energy when directed compassionately towards those who oppose the truth, but many link into this deity for the power to kill enemies and take over kingdoms, in order to keep Egypt great.

The deepest initiations are very challenging, even soul risking procedures that require exceptional courage. The contenders are advised to set up challenges for themselves that they then have to meet. A great deal of preparation and focus is required for this.

Now, beyond time, I am with Sempeth as he travels

to the pyramid to meet Karlesh. The two men hit it off immediately. As kindred spirits, Karlesh can see that Sempeth is the perfect person to pass his deeper knowledge on to.

Sempeth needs this initiation so that the Supreme gods of the earth and heaven can meet in his soul. He knows that deep earth contact will enhance the spiritual gifts in ways that I, too, have found most useful in the spiritual work I do. I am expressing gratitude to him for that.

"Initiation requires precise balance at all stages," Sempeth is told and, to emphasise this, he is taken first to the Queen's chamber for purification. Full initiations were once held there for the more feminine men, who would be taking up advisory positions that did not require the ability to express energy widely. Many of them would dispense compassionate wisdom as seers.

"Most of the officiating priests today are much more cerebral, encouraging potential initiates to appear strong", Karlesh continues. "It is all about image now. These ones are told to orientate themselves in the solar plexus but, when they do that, the whole initiation is certain to be a battle of wills with the shadow forces."

"I deal with the more masculine seekers, the tougher ones. For me to support you in working with the occult power, you must focus intently into the heart and keep this orientation precisely and continuously in place, especially when your mind needs to range free. Do not leave the heart. There is no conflict there. Then you will slide past the shadow ones as they attempt to ensnare you. The heart is the only place to be entirely safe."

The earlier masters of the occult tradition honed their expertise in such areas as alchemy and levitation, over lifetimes of dedication and discipline. They worked together to pass on their power to accomplish great feats of transmutation to a younger man serving his apprenticeship under them. Though not quite at that level of those earlier priests, Karlesh still has an impressive grasp of the time-honoured practices.

Then, four men quietly enter the Queen's chamber, forming a circle in the centre. Karlesh continues to describe the process. "From the King's chamber your inner mind will first descend to here and these priests will send it back further up the pyramid to a room that aligns with the brow chakra in your body. Then you will come down to the throat level where teachings will enter your consciousness which you will retain and later pass on to those you advise. We have mentally established crystal-like energy formations up there, to facilitate this opening up."

"In all chambers of the pyramid, the masculine and feminine energies were segregated and held there. to be merged again, during the relevant stages of the initiation, in ways that are no longer possible."

Sempeth's mind will then gradually come down through the levels, missing this Queen's chamber, which is off-centre, and pass instead through one of two important chambers with a feminine orientation that are just below ground level.

"These four men are very feminine and will, to some degree, provide the balanced stabilising energy needed for your further descent, drawing on the yang within their own natures to enable your liberated soul to continue on down. Later, they will control its assent again after completing the trials you will face down there."

"The significance of those lower chambers has been lost over time and the authorities are intending to seal them off so that the power can be contained and protected, but this is foolish. If used properly, they are a vital part of the network of support needed during the initiations. When your mind reaches that level, ask for female spirits to aid you in your purification."

"Women would be better placed to facilitate this, as their greatest achievements are internal, but they are no longer considered necessary in the higher levels of the priesthood. The priestesses carry out their own initiations with the young women in domestic situations, secretly, so as not to draw attention to themselves. As a feminine man cannot completely replace a woman in the pyramid rituals, some of the most profound initiations are no longer available."

"Remember that the masculine and feminine are aspects of each other. Your male orientation will keep on going down into the earth, as far as it can be supported. The subtle feminine planes are not up there or down there, they're around you, on every level, but you can access them only to the extent that you have entered your heart."

"Each incarnate soul has the free will to choose the direction that it takes, as it evolves, but it must do this with an understanding that the light and the dark lie within each other."

Karlesh then explains that the candidates for initiation get only the level of challenge they are believed to be ready for, which determines the outcome but, pausing to take a deep breath, "not all of the candidates return to their bodies." Then immediately, "All going well, your soul will descend, within what you may experience as a column of light, into the chamber beneath the pyramid."

"All going well?", Sempeth repeats, needing reassurance.

"Mm, yes. Every vile thing that you have ever encountered will try and get at you as you descend, determined to drag you into their haunts and trap you", then laying in on dramatically, "in their seething cauldron of despicable awfulness. They will sweet talk you with promises of eternal life. They will offer to grant you your most fervent desire. And then, if that doesn't succeed, they will threaten your very existence with obliteration if you don't join them. The more you resist, the more intensely they will clutch and claw. If you let fear in, they will pounce on it, snarling and screeching, till you can bear it no longer."

"Could this initiation fail?!", Sempeth cries out. Karlesh is reluctant to continue but eventually looks Sempeth straight in the eyes while admitting that there was one priest, not long ago, a government enforcer with a corrupt view of power, who carried out orders for political reasons.

"Some troublemakers that the authorities wanted out of the way did not survive the initiation process with him. Their souls were trapped in the earth, held there in an energy prison as punishment. He was assassinated eventually. I don't know whether there are others, like him, still in place." Before Sempeth can ask further questions, he continues, "Most of the priests do it with authenticity according to their understanding, though many of the truths have been lost and distorted over time.

The two men stand deepening the eye contact for quite awhile until Sempeth blurts out. "I trust you!"

Karlesh smiles. "I only choose people I know will succeed." After letting that sink in, he escorts Sempeth up to the King's chamber where they are joined by two support priests. The younger man positions himself at the foot of the casket and doesn't speak but Hepu is eager to introduce himself - a very feminine chap, probably much older than he looks, with a broad smile and soulful eyes that Sempeth and I immediately warm to.

"In earlier times", Karlesh explains "a priest and priestess would have jointly taken this role. Later, four priests were needed to oversee this ritual but there are no others that I trust enough to work with me."

Sempeth is then invited to lie in the initiation casket where he is taken through a series of relaxation exercises before gradually surrendering to the hypnotic ritual that the three men are undertaking. Once Sempeth is entranced, I am aware that he is still conscious but only in an inner sense.

There are master spirit guides around Karlish who will direct Sempeth's soul through the initiation process. At times, I feel he is surrounded by more dubious figures as they manoeuvre around him. My mind is relating to the subtle energies and benevolent forms that Sempeth is encountering. I am pleased with the choices he is making.

His mind leaves his body and ascends higher up the

pyramid where it undergoes purification so that the wayward mental attitudes, that could easily take over, are kept in check. He is then subjected to various tests that could seduce him into believing that the ones confronting him are superior beings, entitled to have power over him, along with the more difficult suggestion, that he can have power over others.

Sempeth stills himself, as he is inwardly advised to do, and waits. It is time for his soul mind to be escorted straight down into the chamber beneath the pyramid. A shaft of light shoots down through his crown chakra and the descent begins. On different levels, there are many spirits grappling with the immense pressure of the complex energies being generated there.

Sempeth is held within this light-filled column of consciousness which continues down into the dark chamber beneath the ground, where he is subjected to attacks by the denizens of the gloom who try to entice him to experience one base gratification after another, hoping to gain control of him through this. But it is an illusory world.

Sempeth eases through these trials and reaches the lower chamber where he receives a dispensation of inner Earth energy which enhances his capacity to be simultaneously of Spirit and Earth.

Then he focuses further down into the earth with no deviation from the straight and narrow. The initiation has been an intense experience and now Sempeth's mind returns to the King's chamber with an awakened consciousness similar to what enlightenment had offered me and, most significantly, he is bringing back the capacity to be at peace within the Earth.

Sempeth had learnt much about himself in relation to the work he will subsequently undertake in Thebes where he will take people, he does not always respect, through first stage initiations. His underlying warrior nature, which wants Egypt to be free of imbalance, will come forward when he confronts the rich who are trying to use him to draw in energies of greed and self-justification. The shadow force, beginning to envelop his country, is already intruding into the initiation process.

I am very aware of the extent that my earth energy work has drawn on the strengths attained by Sempeth in his initiation. Further news comes through that Karlesh, in his spirit form, is now working alongside Johosephat as an auxiliary guide. Both will remain with me, right through my earth mission, until I pass to spirit and can join them.

Kalesh stresses, as he did all those centuries ago, that I must never underestimate the power of the disruptive minds and forces that can get in and subtly influence my thoughts, if I let them. The training to avoid this has been mainly carried out in my sleeping hours. My capacity to address the difficulties I still experience in life will determine how well I can progress in subsequent lives.

In earlier stages of my spiritual journey, I faced many forms of self-delusion head-on as they tried to take hold of me. Now, these are returning in quite insidious ways. We earth workers must be ever watchful, even in situations where we would not expect to find trouble.

I know of many potential leaders and spiritual teachers who have been seduced by the temptations of power and wealth and, especially, fame, which they approached initially in good faith. Of course, they said, "I know the dangers. Money, itself, is not evil and my ability to influence many people with the teachings will be used only for the betterment of humanity" – and then, almost without realising it, with justification following justification, they gradually wandered from the path.

Most spiritual teachers emphasise the superiority of 'light and love' over the dark impulses and are not aware that they are actually preventing themselves from reaching down into the sombre and fertile earth where karma and revelation lie side by side. They skirt over the issues when they do not acknowledge and release their part in past wrongdoing, which is often religion-based.

Redemption can be completed when we confront other people who are succumbing to the weaknesses that mirror some of our own, still unresolved, karma. I have noticed that there was one earth monster from previous lives that wasn't addressed by Kalesh in his initiation - spiritual impatience - which certainly came to the fore in that female life of mine, at the time of Ramses II, when she repeatedly challenged the excesses of the upper classes and was soundly punished for it.

This fundamental lack of spiritual understanding was a running theme through many of my subsequent lives when they confronted various powerful leaders of nations and institutions. It is still causing me some frustration when I attempt to stand up to the English hierarchy today, on the inner planes.

"Stick to what is possible," Johosephat stresses before giving me the unwelcome news that I have still more of this kind of challenge to face in this current life and, after a pause, the two lives to follow.

It is obvious that Luxor is finished for me. My final jaunt to Egypt will be to the Great Pyramid to replenish and extend that early pyramid initiation so that I can get ready to face further challenges.

❧

My loyal friend, Sukti, is first to sign up and then Joseph whom I believe was Thutmose II himself. In this present life, he is a very conflicted soul, wanting power but having none. This is a very select group.

A friend with travel connections in Cairo, sets up our accommodation there and arranges a private tour to the pyramid. We add Barakat to our group and, the following day, five of us fly there with great expectations. Our accommodation is just off the main square, the site of anti-government protests recently.

Early the following morning, the scheduled driver arrives to pick us up. He is very friendly until he tells us that going inside the Great Pyramid isn't part of the package.

I hold back the harsh response that wants to snap out of me but a ferocious scowl is enough to tell him how furious I am. "You can always go into one of the other pyramids if it doesn't work out," he says, still not realising how important this is to us.

He quickly adds that we can queue at 10 am in the hope that extra tickets will be released. We secure the last batch of day passes available, just before the cut-off time of 2 pm. My frustration is released and I gallop towards the entrance with Barakat close behind.

Inside, we first pass along the cramped passages leading up to the grand gallery, the largest cavity in this intricately inspired creation but, when we reach it, I am totally unprepared for the shock that pierces through me, at just how vast and awe inspiring it is.

What little light there is, reflects off the sombre sepia walls. Spirits from the past are everywhere, whispering to anyone sensitive enough to hear them. I can feel an almost irresistible force drawing me down into the underworld as we prepare to climb upwards. Strange that - but then I remember the soul descent that is to come.

I adjust to being in a heightened reality like no other, with none of my normal securities in place. I am trying to make out what the people ahead of me, making the long ascent to the King's Chamber, are calling out to their friends below, but the walls deaden any connection with them. Only the boom, boom drum of silence.

At last, it is our turn to climb the strutted boardwalk towards this magical room. I am the first to burst in. It turns out to be a musty, featureless space. We have no experienced guide with us, so I ask my inner companions to tell me what lies behind this bare, grey-walled disappointment. They do not respond.

I very slowly move to the initiation casket and there I am, inside it already. I try to join my subtle self. "Wait!", an inner voice demands, "this is not a game." So, I stand motionless and enter my heart from where everything must be directed.

Suddenly, the ceiling dissolves. A night sky canopies the room. The stars vary in brightness, as they always did, but one particularly stands out, my favourite, winking at me. As a child, I had said "I came from there." Now, I am absolutely certain. But, immediately, "When?" follows, and "Why?"

Johosephat scolds me from the other side. "That will come later. Focus on your soul journey ahead."

I wait and, after merging with my subtle self, the two of us are sucked upwards through a succession of chambers. I am revisiting the initiation my former life went through, so that I can be fully imbued with the heightened awareness that he is passing on to me. This takes no time at all. I pause to allow a deepening of that experience. The rays, streaming down from the night sky, fill my heart with effervescent bubbles that dart into many parts of my body.

The universal nature of the experience becomes clear. Although standing in a very solid room, I am a space traveller making a direct connection with my home planet. Then suddenly, the imagined sky clouds over.

My soul counterpart and I begin to descend, pausing briefly at each level. One is a spherical energy space, a short distance from the Queen's chamber. It could be an undiscovered physical chamber representing the sacral chakra but, more likely, it only exists on more subtle levels. I know little about the sacral because Maisie had told me to entirely avoid this chakra.

"It isn't safe", she said. "You never know what will emerge from there to waylay you."

I feel now that this was one area she should have explored in herself but that would have been difficult for a woman in those more sexually repressed times. I am registering it as a multi-faceted creative space that I will certainly be exploring in myself later on.

At ground level, the descent shudders to a sudden stop.

"Is this as far as I can go?" That would be a disappointment.

"Of course not", comes to me, "Stay with your inner focus and wait till the resistance gives way."

I comply but, as usual, it takes quite a bit longer than I feel comfortable with. It is like being in a vacuum. No movement. All sensations tightly suppressed. Scary. It could be what death is like at first.

"Slow your breathing", I keep telling myself. "Go to your heart and surrender." I am on the brink and know that I mustn't give up. Suddenly then, the downward trajectory lurches on and I am breathing deeply again.

The next stop involves the two feminine chambers, a little beneath the surface of the earth, that have still not been discovered by archaeologists. I know that, by keeping myself aligned to my central channel, I will avoid all of the negativity waiting to envelop me.

Though I expect many demons to be waiting in the subterranean chamber that follows, strangely enough, there is no apprehension and, on reaching this dreaded monstrous pit, they are nowhere to be seen.

"This is not your initiation", my spirit supporters remind me. "It has all been done. Your task is to venture further down beyond anything he achieved so that you can work deeper inside the earth when the need arises."

All around, there is much activity, some quite threatening, but I am held safe and detached within it. The secret is to achieve heart balance and then there is no need for protection. This is the vital lesson I learnt with Maisie that has been invaluable since. So, I focus again into my heart and the descent continues.

We pass through that underground chamber unscathed, and down one more level. There is a pulsating energy source straight ahead and I notice various friendly gnome-like figures beside me and, further off, some rather more powerful subterranean beings I have not encountered before. In what is rather like gazing into a crystal ball, I can see a river with early Egyptian sailing boats on it. I look directly at this and the scene disappears.

"Can't you learn that lesson, Greg", I snap at myself. "Keep everything on the periphery. Sense, don't look at what is there." This vital ability is enabling me to remain unscathed, as some Luciferian beings seem to be seeking a head-on clash with me, that they could easily win if I engaged with them.

This subterranean world is filled with patches of light, no full-on intensity. Figures are discretely emerging out of the gloom noticed only when they wish it. I sense one approaching on my left side. Male, probably, but unlikely to be human. I feel an affinity, though, and am immensely comfortable when he positions himself beside me. No thoughts pass between us. He just wants me to know that he is there, and I sense that we will be together on other journeys I will make into the earth later on.

I notice that my forgotten counterpart self is feeling uncomfortable and wants to return to the King's Chamber. I am becoming more aware that, to be a truly spiritual person, it is necessary to split into a dual nature, one earthly and one of the ethers, the true partnership affinity, with a distinct division of roles and no competition. I must provide the focus and discipline and he, the free creative expression.

I then approach another casket, a counterpart of the one in the King's chamber, and my subtle self is placed in it for the final phase of this ritual. I sense that there are two more levels below this, for the really advanced initiations, but this is all I can handle now.

Back in the King's Chamber, I am aware that my friend Barakat has been keeping people away from my side of the casket. I look up and see both attendants coming over. They've been very sensitive to my need to be left alone but it is now closing time.

֍

On reaching the airport, we are told that our plane has been cancelled and there is no replacement possible before mid-morning. As we are scheduled to return to London later that day, I instinctively put on one of the dramatic turns I use to get my own way. I stagger around, loudly proclaiming how disgraceful it is and demanding to see the airport manager. A 2.30 am flight miraculously materialises.

This kerfuffle has temporarily sent the events in the pyramid to the back of my mind where they stay. There are so many goodbyes to say to Barakat's family and the other villagers that I've established warm relationships with, over the years, for I know this is my final visit to Egypt.

As the plane soars above Luxor, I feel relief that the obsession that brought me here, so many times, is no longer active. I may have to link the four lives in Thebes with something much earlier. I am now intuiting that I visited the Giza region long before the Great Pyramid was constructed.

So many questions to grapple with before I can link up each phase of my earth journey. There seems to be a black hole in my memory and I sense that something happened in this earlier life that brought a great turbulence into my destiny progress - but any further revelations will have to wait until I am ready to receive them.

11

Returning to Lemuria

2005

After returning from Egypt, there is much to do to keep the Helios charity going. Maisie had taken me back to the Akhenaten period. At 96, her mind is failing and I realise that, in this life, her main objective has been to channel her Pharaoh son and sort out her ego-bound ex-Pharaoh husband. In going to the Great Pyramid, I have opened the door to earlier times.

I am now absolutely convinced that I had a life, many thousands of years before the one in Thebes. I ask her when that was.

"It was when Atlantis was in decline," is her response, which raises far more questions than it answers. She is unable to elaborate further.

I visit many unsuitable organisations in my search for further information about Atlantis" until I hear of the Spirit Release Foundation, a gathering of people who can liberate trapped spirits, as Maisie did in her rescue work.

On attending their Summer conference, I am greeted by the chair of their board, Tony Neate. I could easily mistake him for a much-loved country pastor, but I very soon see that his unassuming nature masks a man of steely determination with a great deal of missionary zeal.

In our first conversation, he says, "We have some very accomplished practitioners in this most important field, who do not feel they have to be in the limelight. While the coming Aquarian Age is a time of the individual, the cult of personality is a Piscean trait."

He adds that he is a trance medium and founder of 'The School of Channelling.' Can this be the man I am looking for? That is settled when he tells me that his guide is Helio Arconophus who was a high priest of Atlantis. He invites me to his home in Malvern.

That evening, I locate some books in my library on Atlantis that I've never read and yes, all but two of them contain channelled lectures by Tony Neate's guide, H.A. It was absolutely right that I did not make contact with him earlier. I needed to continue my spiritual and psychic development with Maisie and follow the Egyptian path.

I've read them all by the time we meet but I'm still rather wary of the content. An advanced civilisation that existed thousands of years before Jesus, on a collection of islands in the Atlantic, which sank into the sea after volcanic eruptions. It seems a mite bit fantastic but all doubts are put aside when my meditations confirm that this indeed is the man I am to work with next.

From the station, he takes me up into the Malvern hills where I take in the exceptional views.

"This is the most ancient part of the country", he tells me. "We don't get many people coming here, thank goodness. It would be awful if it were like Glastonbury which has become filled with people determined to draw on the energies for themselves."

He then takes me to a lavish flat where his wife, Ann, is waiting and the three of us chat amiably for a while, agreeing that the time of the big religions is over. Small groups, with no dominant leader, must generate the essential spiritual activity that will build secure foundations for the new Earth. Everyone will have special gifts that they share.

Certainly, in the Peacemakers Circle, the power we generate is far more than the sum of the individual contributions.

Tony gives me an unpublished collection of the guide's teachings, 'New Dimensions in Healing', full of practical hints and new perspectives for anyone working in this field. I promise to edit this to get it ready for publication.

After a delicious meal, Tony settles himself, closes his eyes, and I wait for the 'great man' to speak. "Greetings dear friend. I do indeed come to you from the heart. Balance is everything in spiritual work. Many people find it difficult to understand that the light and the shadow are essential parts of the whole and must be kept in harmony, not polarised as you see so often today. The line in the Great Invocation – 'Seal the door where evil dwells' - is completely misguided. It will only break out more destructively, in another form, later on."

When he asks for questions, I choose the most difficult. "My healing has become more and more heart-centred, in line with the Piscean energies. What shifts are needed for me to move into the air-orientated Aquarian age of the mind."

"This is not the first time you have been present at the change of the ages hoping to bring things into a much better state. Always, you left with a heavy heart for you expected it to be achieved in just one lifetime. Humanity's lack of understanding of the planet's ills will take much longer to remedy. You must face life with the same positivity and immediacy as your heart does, drawing in the past, cleansing it, and projecting unconditional love into the future. Then, when you pass into the spirit world, you will have done as much as you can in this life."

Feeling slightly judged, I quickly change the subject. "Having read some of your ideas on Atlantis, I want to know how I fit into this. How many Atlantean lives did I have?"

"Seven", is the unexpected reply. "The fourth one was at its peak when the technology they developed was truly amazing. The seventh was right at the end."

"I was in Libya then." This was a question masquerading as a statement.

"Yes. You weren't ready for the higher power and abilities. It declined after that and by the end, they had let the heavy earth energies undermine everything and it really went disastrously awry. The priests were too caught up in their little world of elevated thought and were unaware that, in the distant hamlets, degraded practices and black magic were being practised."

I want to probe further but Tony comes out of trance. On my next visit, a month later, Tony enthusiastically takes out a massive file full of extra teachings on Atlantis that, he says, are no less astounding than what I've already read.

I take this home and start to edit it down into a second book, 'Secrets of Planet Earth' which puts the various early civilisations into a context, presenting the more esoteric concepts and information in a way that makes them relevant to the life and needs of readers today. Without that, they will merely encourage a fantasy world of a kind so prevalent in modern spirituality.

I continue my monthly visits determined to understand how my Egyptian lives followed on from the earlier Atlantean ones. I ask where Atlantis was exactly.

"Fueteventura, in the Canary Islands, is the closest you can get to the epi-centre of the Atlantean civilisation", Ann responds. "Tony and I have been going there twice a year since 2001, to teach and give readings."

For a 76-year-old, Tony's energy and commitment are impressive. His important ground-breaking work is based on his philosophy of humility and unconditional love but he is having difficulty in fully grounding the energies and this may become a serious issue for him.

He has aroused the spirit of Atlantis in me but I want to know if I was in Egypt at the end.

"No, in one of the satellite areas."

That was definitely Libya. Left on my own, I tune into him. He is a passionate, single-minded man who entered the priesthood with his younger brother, who was an earlier life of my colleague, Robin Baldock. Naturally, he is expecting the senior priests to encourage the divine consciousness that is awakening in his heart. Instead, my chap uncovers persistent spiritual imbalance in the community and, behind that, the systematic corruption going on.

The four senior priests profess to be doing God's will but they are using occult practices to manipulate the lives and soul progress of their young charges in unhealthy ways. Sexual activity is forbidden and we know where that leads to in any priesthood.

My past life's warrior nature takes over. He explains, in vivid detail, exactly what this corrupt band are doing, to anyone who will listen. This leads to a revenge of the kind usually meted out by ruthless people whose authority is threatened.

The two brothers are sitting bowed in prayer when two guards storm in. They look up and return to their meditations. Though not resisting, their hands are bound anyway. They are dragged to a room in the complex where only the senior priests are allowed. The four initially try to put them at ease, so that they can extract information.

I am merging here with that past life so that I can understand the full impact of what happened. My brother is too frightened to say anything but, in standing up to them, I rather foolishly, rail against their personal failings when asked to confess mine.

Gagged now, they proceed to carry out what they had intended to do, without the satisfaction of seeing me grovel and plead for mercy. I am now in the graveyard where there is only one casket poised beside a hole in the ground. They are not going to send my brother to the same fate. He is forced to watch so that he will not cause them any trouble in the future.

I am being placed in the coffin which is sealed before being lowered into the grave. I begin to realise just how catastrophic this will be for my entire incarnational line. Dying violently was common enough in those days but this is a planned ritual. They are making sure that I won't bother them again in any subsequent life. It will a prolonged death because there is a pipe from the coffin to the surface for air to get in.

I hear earth being thrown onto the coffin. For three days, their incantations are energetically controlled and vicious. Eventually, they believe that they have sealed my soul in bonds that it cannot ever escape from. Water is then poured down the pipe, so that I will drown. As life ebbs away, I experience a soul implosion coinciding with the upheavals in the sea around the main Atlantis settlement, as the elements buffet and finally sink that fated island.

Though it was a failure for them, it interrupted my entire evolutionary progress. I could not incarnate again on Earth for over 7,000 years.

Many more questions flood but the one I ask Tony is, "Are my Atlantean lives, the first I had on the planet?"

"No, your earth journey began long before."

"But where?"

No answer. Those spoilsports never tell me anything until I have already worked it out for myself.

According to his teachings, the Atlanteans had originally migrated from Lemuria when that civilisation ended. That settles it. I'm not wasting any more time on the Atlantis debacle. Lemuria is earlier and I have to go there. Perhaps this is where I first settled on the planet.

I like to work with maps, and always use triangles to identify where the main concentrations of energy are located. My colleague, Robin, joins me in the search for clues. He is drawn to Southern India but this is north of the equator and a hunch tells me that Lemuria was mainly in the southern hemisphere.

Africa is where the natural Earth people evolved from. This is now well accepted. So, we move across to South America. Not Peru, we decide, before scanning down to the very repressed Chile. Yes, that is where the second point on the Lemurian triangle is situated. I am directed to the mountains above Santiago.

On to the final one. After deciding that New Zealand is not a large enough land mass, we switch across to Australia. I immediately think of Ayre's Rock, now known as Uluru, its Aboriginal name, but no, it has to be on the west coast. At the top, there is the vast, romantic Kimberley wilderness that I dreamt of visiting as a child, the source of great primeval power.

My focus then zooms down to the capital, Perth, which is on the same latitude as Santiago. I let out an excited squeal, "There it is. My next place to go!" We have completed the triangle, though a very unbalanced one.

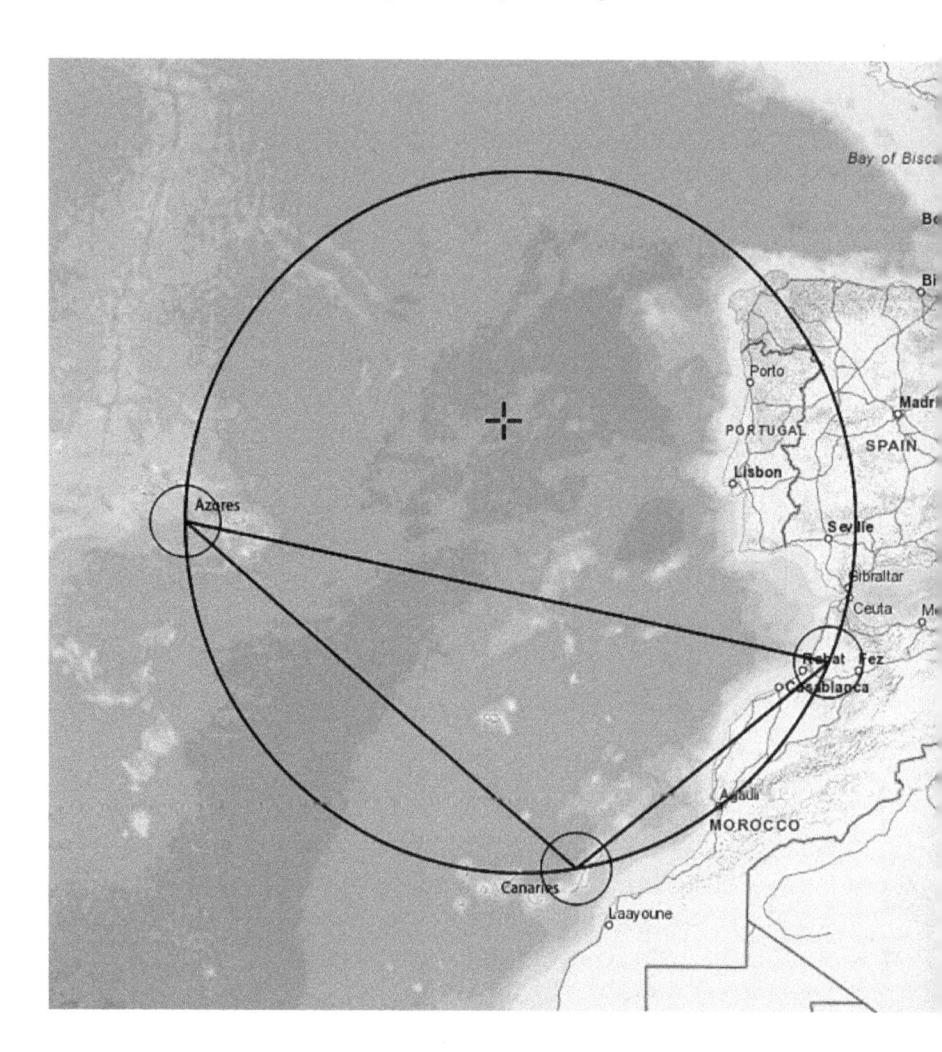

2006

Over the following months, I ponder many questions. The most important is, "Where did the Lemurians come from?" The answer hits me almost immediately, "My star!"

A week in the library barely uncovers a glimpse of the impact that this celestial body has had on many cultures.

I already know that Sirius, the brightest star in the sky, is located in the constellation Canis Major and is known as the "dog star". It is over twenty times brighter than our Sun and twice as large. Its blue-white aura has fascinated astronomers since the dawn of time and it has featured in the mythology surrounding both tribal groupings and the more sophisticated cultures who believed that Sirius provided a higher, almost god-like power to our Sun.

The ancient Egyptian calendar system was based on the heliacal rising of Sirius that occurred just before the annual Summer flooding of the Nile. The star's celestial movement was also observed and revered by the ancient Greeks, Sumerians, Babylonians and countless other civilizations.

Modern secret societies such as the Freemasons, the Rosicrucians and the Golden Dawn all attribute the utmost importance to Sirius.

The Great Pyramid of Giza was built in alignment with Sirius and, significantly, the light behind the All-Seeing Eye on the American dollar bill is shining right above the Pyramid. A radiant tribute to Sirius is in the pockets of millions of citizens.

Robin and I reach across galaxies in an attempt to link the Lemurian triangle back to Sirius, but this isn't it. We also reject the very faint white dwarf star, Sirius B, which surprised astronomers when it was discovered in 1844. We move on to a third, even smaller, companion star and there it is. The Lemurians definitely came from a planet revolving around Sirius C. But why?

To answer this, we are taken back 100,000 years which, of course, is nothing in the evolution of the Universe, but the Sirian planet had gone completely out of balance to the point where its very existence was threatened.

Every planet in a solar system is essential. Were the concentrated energies deep within that planet to burst out and break apart the physical structure, it would have seriously upset the cohesion of the entire planetary system and set evolution back millions of years. Something had to be done.

It is difficult to imagine a get-together of the ones who oversee the universe but let us accept that a meeting of those great minds did occur.

Each of the stars and planets actively interacts with the others on many levels simultaneously. Solar systems have their own collective identity and free will. Nothing can be imposed by the godhead, so help had to come from elsewhere on the physical level. Many solar systems were looked at to find a planet that could take on some of the unbalanced Sirian energy without disturbing its integrity too much.

They chose Earth, which is the central, heart energy of our solar system, and therefore the most balanced. By taking on a part of the negativity, the load of the troubled Sirian planet would be relieved. Of course, it would affect the integrity of our own planetary arrangement to some degree, with Earth taking the brunt, but this was felt to be manageable.

So, it came to pass. That planet was saved from extinction and Earth was left with serious balance problems and needing to gradually reintegrate itself. Normally, the energies, gently oscillating at the core of the planet, would 'breath' towards the surface with smooth manageable evolutionary steps. Instead, the inherited imbalance emphasised the higher frequencies, the Father God, and this meant that all life forms would have to struggle to keep their evolution fully grounded.

Indeed, exploitation from above was widespread from

the outset. The predatory nature of the meat-eaters in the animal kingdom is one example of this problem and, of course, our own warlike natures forever fighting for supremacy.

Fast forward to fifteen thousand years ago. Planet Earth, saddled with this exacting responsibility, has become somewhat retarded in its evolution. The natural earthlings, mostly from Africa, live simple lives aligned to the earth. They do not open up to the intellectual parts of themselves very much. A massive scientific outpouring lay ahead and humanity needed help to evolve its moral strength and overall spiritual tone, to be ready for this.

So, the dual-natured Christ consciousness approached the Sirian oversoul, which had moved on thanks to the help it had received from Earth, and requested a migration of some of its more capable inhabitants to directly influence and hasten the evolution of humanity here. Millions responded, mainly in spiritual families of around a thousand souls and the first wave of these volunteers incarnated, soon after, to the three points of the Lemurian triangle.

This is a lot to take in. Before taking off in early March for an initial six-week reconnoitre, Robin and I divine that the local Lemurian heart energy is centred within the wealthy Darlington area in the hills to the east of Perth. My mind gallops on, as it usually does. I have a vision where I establish a home for my later years, six months in London and six months there, avoiding the winters in both places. Future settled.

When I arrive at Darlington, my map lights up at Glen Road near a scout hall. That is where I must go. However, the Sunday bus service lands me far from there. The universe often tells me to exercise more and it is great to be back stretching my legs in the Australian bush.

As I walk slowly down Glen Road, no visions of past events are welcoming me until I reach my destination when a surge of activity begins. I am propelled away from the scout hall, up past a deserted bush kindergarten to a higher position with a marvellous view. It is significant that children are always found around heart chakra points.

It is an uneven area with patches of dense clumps of grass and a few large rocks dotted around but no ancient Lemurian city. Then, suddenly, I enter into that time reality where my former self is standing in front of me. He invites me to enter a round ceremonial room where a group of robed men and women are gathered around a large square bench in the middle. He impresses on me that it is an observatory though there are no telescopes.

They are gazing into a large crystal. Streams of light are being directed into it from windows high up, twelve of them, each with a different coloured tinge.

He was not part of that group, though he did draw on cosmic energies from there for his healing. They had a much more sophisticated and far-reaching understanding than our scientists today. As I relax further into my heart, I discern a rich level of thought energy operating on subtle levels that explains something of how they operated.

My early life takes me to another building nearby, where he worked - and this is a surprise - in genetic engineering. The Lemurians had come to the planet to speed up the progress of human evolution but the Sirian planet is not balanced in the heart. Its natural orientation is halfway between the heart and throat levels. By nature, the French are possibly the closest in temperament to many of those from that planet, which says a lot about why they had difficulty adjusting to the earth's energies while remaining peaceful.

They initially incarnated into bodies that were genetically unable to allow the required maturity of expression. They had to gradually modify their own genetic composition so that later generations could manifest the higher spiritual abilities that they had on their home planet.

Now, fully into that timeframe, I realise that they are naively expecting that it will take only four or five generations for the Lemurian mission to complete. They are certainly re-awakening and introducing cultural ideas from their Sirian memory but they are introducing genetic changes in themselves that are not fully resonant with this planet.

Their intention is well-meaning but their understanding, projected forward into their own later lives in the Atlantean period, shows them still manipulating the genes of the local people, and much more aggressively, unaware that this is causing a dangerous schism between mind and body.

The Lemurian experiments were rather traumatising for the indigenous populations who lost contact with their own evolutionary source. This regrettable karmic error, that he and his group of scientists made then, is still with me, motivating much of the reparation that I have been engaged with in this present life.

We move towards the education complex where women teachers are playing with the younger ones outside. At the age of 12 or 13, the men take over. Further over is the living quarters for the priests. A snake slithering nearby, in present time, forces me to retreat towards a campfire area that the scouts use, with a view across a small ravine. Looking down, though it is late Summer, there is water running through it, sheltered by masses of bamboo. The map refers to it as the Nyaania creek.

Above it, on the other side, there are several large smooth rocks used for earth-orientated ceremonies. The large rock is where the men would meet and, lower down, there is the women's much smaller area. As it is getting late and the last bus cannot be guaranteed, I do not go across there on this first visit.

I am already intending to return to Perth, so I look at the monthly new age broadsheet, Nova, hoping to find individual seekers, personal development groups and spiritual gatherings to link up with. There isn't actually a lot going on, other than seminars by respected overseas teachers.

I visit their organiser, Jill Mattioli. After glancing at

my credentials, she agrees to organise one of my groups when I next come to town.

The following Saturday, I meet the dowser, Tony Henshaw, at his Natural Resonance Study Group. He agrees to help me with the maps and we team up to divine the location of all the other chakra points in the Darlington area, except the base one which is totally unresponsive to his pendulum. We visit them all in order, starting with the crown which is within a compact tree setting above the Boya quarry.

With the power there funnelling straight up, we look to the sky directly above us, focussing in on a large single cloud. It dissolves away completely. Two hawks begin to circle around above us. We make mental contact with them and they oblige by swooping down very close to us for more than ten minutes, before shooting off at an angle.

Over the next few weeks, I visit all of the spiritualist churches in the metropolitan area. The mediums are well-meaning, but unbelievably naive. The last one on the list is in Fremantle, the major port city located at the mouth of the Swan River, 27 miles south of Perth. It was the first area settled by the early colonists and, today, is known for a very lively arts scene.

Alighting from the train there, I am propelled to the dock front where another déjà vue surprise awaits me. As I stand looking out to sea, I am back in the very early days of the settlement. It is 1838. I have just disembarked from a large sailing boat as a five-year-old boy. My elder sister is holding my hand.

This is to be my home but my parents are already regretting the trip. How primitive the township looks. Being quite well off, they are soon accepted into the social circles of that day. We have three servants and my sister and I go to a small Anglican school nearby.

In my teens, there is a girl I fancy from a newly arrived family. We marry some years later. My parents are a God-fearing couple and I am expected to support those less privileged than we are. However, when I see how appallingly the aboriginal community is treated, I announce that they are the ones I want to help. Mater and Pater are not pleased. Their Christian charity extends only so far and my wife can't even bear to get close to them. "Smelly creatures," she snooty sniffs, "you never know what they've been up to."

I am determined to set up a charity to help them find employment and healthcare. Cut off from their natural surroundings and their herbal remedies, without any natural immunity, many develop serious eye conditions and their sight is deteriorating. I try to raise money but am seen as deluded by many of my peers. They are ignorant savages hardly worth bothering with.

I become increasingly dejected, feeling that my life of privilege prevents me from following my calling. My wife forces me to attend social events where alcohol flows freely. When she leaves me for another man, I turn to serious drinking and, at the age of 29, my body gives up.

I don't drink now but, in Perth, the aboriginal issue is clearly karma that I must address.

The Fremantle Spiritualist Church is nearby and I meet up with its young chairman, Paul Smith. We talk at some length after the rather unconvincing service. I only have two more days left, so it will not be until the next trip that our friendship can develop.

The Second Visit

I am much more prepared when I return in autumn that year. Jill, my new agent, has organised one of my 'Communicating with Confidence' courses for the following Saturday, in a local church hall. There are six people booked but she hasn't taken deposits.

On arriving there, I set up the circle and we wait for the participants to turn up. None of them does. A disappointment but, soon after, Paul arrives. His other engagement has been cancelled at the last minute. Clearly, a good man and, as I will discover, exceptionally loyal. He volunteers to ferry me around to the various sites.

My main task, on this trip, is to find the elusive base chakra. That is solved when Jill tells me about a group she'd belonged to, run by the medium, May Smith, and her doctor husband, Eric. May had channelled information about a great city in the Eastern hills, Astroeth, meaning "City of Light", and this was located a few miles from Darlington.

They subsequently bought the house and land around it where they were joined by a scientist, interested in anti-matter, who was able to project himself into the past psychically. He saw blue-robed figures poring over maps of the ancient city. When other people were drawn in later, they started 'The Seekers Group' to study the teachings coming through.

An eight-foot square temple remains from that early time when it hosted many spiritual groups but, since the seventies, the new owner, again a doctor, has used it as a tool shed.

Jill gives me some of May Smith's writings which I take back to my digs to digest. Paul agrees to take me there the following weekend. I ring the present owner asking for permission but get the unexpected, "Another of you cranks. Don't let me catch you on my land."

"You won't," I reply. Then, much more forcefully, "I can guarantee that!"

Leaving the car at the top of the hill, we go down the steep, water creviced, dirt road until we notice a low flat rock setting to the left. Looking further up the hill there is a substantial rock formation with gum trees clustered around. We head straight towards it.

The doctor's house is further up the hill. We make sure he doesn't spot us when exploring his side of the outcrop. The forbidden nature of this adventure makes it all the more exciting.

After leaping over a log, almost squashing a couple of gecko lizards hissing at us, we reach a sunken area, cut out of the side of the hill. Some of the rocks are perfectly shaped rectangular blocks. Jill has told me of attempts, by a quarrying outfit, to cut the rock up further but the machinery refused to work and it was abandoned. Also, the dials on low-flying aircraft apparently went haywire when passing overhead.

I am not expecting to encounter any negative spirit entities. They tend to keep well away from me but there are several very aggressive ones outside a protective shield around the site. They definitely don't want us to go further.

"Why not?" I ask, but their only response is a seething sound.

"Ignore them", I say to Paul, who is also aware of their presence. "They can't get at us."

We dance from rock to rock towards a large flat, very prominent one, jutting out, where we meditate. This special place invokes incredibly intense pulsating energies and as I focus intently through the rock into the earth below, using the skills I learnt in the Great Pyramid, a thin ray of violet energy is released straight into the base of my spine going up through my crown chakra towards the cosmos.

I come into my element at base chakra sites. Perhaps it's in my genes to feel completely at home with the energies and the elemental beings who live beneath the natural Australian landscape. I can very easily slip into other realities with them.

I am suddenly aware of my spirit guide, Johosephat, taking advantage of this perfect setting for a reunion. I ask him why I don't experience this inner freedom anywhere in England.

"You will eventually, but there is a restriction in that country that holds everyone within very tight boundaries. Few there want to go into the earth. There is too much unresolved history in the way. Soon, you will reach down far enough to dislodge some very important blocked karma there."

Then, I am stunned to see the old man, who came to comfort my four-year-old self in his bedroom, stepping out of the rock face beside me. I can hardly believe it. My mind leaps everywhere, unable to accept the enormity of this meeting. Am I imagining it?

I am crying now, discretely, not wanting Paul to know what a sop I am. I slow my breathing down until the old man is right beside me. His words are exactly what I need to hear.

"It is time to put the pieces of your spiritual journey into a coherent whole, so that we can work closely, two souls in perfect harmony, on a very special mission. Before long you'll realise who I am and why we are together. Will you venture with me now?" This is a redundant question. I am raring to go.

"In your mind, place a sphere around this entire rock formation. You are standing on an energy floor between the hemispheres."

As I do this, my psychic awareness is boosted substantially. I look side-on, as usual, to the centre of the dome. He is there now, giving me his mandatory world-weary smile. Although he doesn't live in physical form, I know that he fully understands humanity and my difficulties.

He beckons me towards an instrument panel in the

centre of the dome, operated by the mind. He wants me to focus in on a destination while being open to anything appearing there.

"There is no need to travel to it," he says. "If you look intently and intend to be in a particular place in outer space, by surrendering to it, that's where you'll be." I try the much closer Perth mall and it works.

He then suggests that I project straight down through my base chakra into the rock beneath my feet, first choosing how far down I want to be.

"If you aren't ready to go that deep, you will immediately feel it", he says.

This resonates with my experiences in the great pyramid and I know that I mustn't overreach myself in this work, a tendency of mine. Even so, a shock goes through the right side of my head and I have to adjust my focus. I wait and this is followed by a serene confidence that, if I listen to my heart, I will be told what is possible in advance and I won't make myself unnecessarily vulnerable.

I focus intently deep into my heart, making contact with the inner earth beings who wish to work with me. I withdraw all expectations. There is a sudden expansion and I am in a natural world with everything clearly defined and organised. There are two figures beside me with a reptilian feel to them. "Are they my lizards?"

"No", I am told, "We are undines, water spirits."

"Like mermaids?", I ask.

They laugh in response. "We inner earth beings represent the elements in ways you would find hard to understand. Think metal and rock, natural gas, subterranean water and lava."

Other figures are morphing out of the semi-tangible forms on the periphery of my vision where the trees were. One of them, suddenly, is right next to me. This is old hat stuff. The need to travel between one place and another is not their reality but I want to do it with them. My mentor talks me through the process.

"Where do you want to be?"

"The heart centre on Glen Road."
"Good, but which part exactly?"
"On the large rock."
"See it, but not in your mind. Place it inside your heart. Don't try to make it happen. It just needs a subtle intention and you'll be there automatically."

It works. Fascinating.

"This kind of travel was once physically possible – and it will be again when your human compatriots wake up."

I ask the obvious question, "Was this where I had my first life on the planet?"

"No", comes the reply, "your second."

I don't bother asking, "Then, where is the first?" for I know the answer will be, "Have patience, my son."

"You can access different levels with a slight shift of perspective. There is the heart region within the earth where I go when I need to rest." He extends his hands towards me and the two of us sink straight down into the earth without any of the resistances I encountered in the Great Pyramid. He holds me energetically until we reach a tranquil, secluded glen. There is something not tangible about it and I'm not altogether comfortable there. Everything is in constant flux.

I notice an aura outline around the various forms and the dominant colour is green, but with other colours coming and going that are generating perfect harmony. His deep sympathy overwhelms me, as it did my young self. I am on the verge of crying when he steps in and fills a place in my heart that has been empty for so long.

He tells me that some five hundred years after my incarnation here, the Lemurian community began to diminish in spiritual understanding when the planetary power supporting them waned. They lost their more profound magical abilities. Group cohesion suffered as a result.

I can see this and when I move forward in time, there are people running around terrified. An earthquake is destroying their city.

"These violent earth shifts often come along when the energy withdraws."

I can see that the city extends right across to the rock formation. The dip down to the creek was caused by a fissure opening up during the quake.

"Almost half the community died at that time. The surviving members moved to this base chakra area and started again. They continued for several hundred more years before the Lemurian experiment came to an end. The spirit had departed."

"As you return to the present, you will learn how to negotiate the turbulence and conflicts that we have to move through when we come close to the earth. It is getting worse. We do wish you would stop."

After returning to the almost here and now, my old mentor says his goodbyes. "Explore this ancient land lovingly and it will reveal all the secrets you are seeking. Bless you, my son." He returns to the rock face and dissolves into it.

The potency and diversity of these experiences are enough to launch a new phase of my work. I can now vividly connect to the realms deep within the earth. I am beginning to collaborate with the beings living down there and, already, I feel entirely safe with them.

The following weekend, Paul and I go to the Glen Road site. We clamber down and cross to the ceremonial rock formation on the other side of the Nyaania creek. Once there, I place my usual sphere around us and establish a direct link to the collective soul of the local aboriginal community.

I notice twelve tribesmen around us, at a distance, watching. I can sense others in the nearby bushes, reluctant to approach, still unable to throw off the karma when they were dispossessed from their land and killed, some of them, for there was a massacre on this site.

Then my own aboriginal guardian spirit encourages me to go with him to more subtle levels. There are three, with a single dominant colour in each: green, ochre and gold.

They appear as abstract landscapes, linked to complex patterns, each with a different purpose.

On returning to the rock, I notice that Paul has wandered off. From there, I am able to send energies to the tribesmen surrounding me which, I know, will help them work closer to those elementals who live inside the rock. I am also creating a bridge between their time and the present.

The full redemption is not yet possible for the atrocities carried out by the English invaders, which has been compounded by the ongoing lack of respect for the aboriginal people. This resonates with my own failure to help them, in that earlier incarnation. I know in my heart that I must do something in this life to work out that wrongdoing. There and then, I decide to set up a charity catering to the needs of the indigenous community. It will be called the 'Nyaania Community'.

This decision fills my heart with immense enthusiasm. Perthect. I fly out on a mega-high for everything is falling into place as if predetermined.

12

Atlantis at last
2012

It has been a rather uneventful year, so far, but we are approaching, the much-hyped, 21st December when, according to the Maya, that sunrise will mark the first time in 26,000 years that the ecliptic position of our Sun is in conjunction with the intersection of the Milky Way at the Galactic Centre. This, they say, will open a portal allowing cosmic energies to flow through, purifying the earth, while raising humanity to a higher vibration. It will be the beginning of the next World Age accompanied by a powerful influx of Stellar energies and changes to the fabric of time. Wow!

Many new age people are expecting a complete resolution of the past plus some kind of ascension for those especially honoured people, themselves, who will be lifted up to the heights without having done the spiritual hard graft to earn it.

So, I must avoid the hooey surrounding that day for although I feel that a heightened consciousness is already available to us, this is bringing up more of our deep-seated karma, built up over the centuries, that still needs resolution.

As I see it, the arrival of the Aquarian age heralds a long, steep climb to the ultimate peak of advanced spiritual capability that we Sirians are working towards, at least a thousand years ahead. By then, we will have addressed the aggressive behaviour, inherited from the civilisations we participated in, that is still rampaging around the planet today. A substantial collective enlightenment is needed before we can manifest and sustain a mature and vibrant world.

I certainly still have much to do in this and future lifetimes before I will have addressed and rectified enough of my past blunders that are still preventing me from working fully with the more refined energies and capabilities.

I am aware that everything I once believed to be blocking my spiritual progress is an illusion but, of course, some of the past lives, who initiated those convoluted mindsets, are still there, trying to convince me that it is all real.

This transition period, from one era to another, requires a synthesis of two quite different astrological signs and, as a child of the Piscean age, I am still locked into thought structures that prevent me from fully embracing and grounding the more cerebral Aquarian consciousness as it intensifies around me.

We have entered the age of the individual where the mind and emotions are becoming increasingly separate. I have not succumbed to a smartphone addiction where the mental processes rule. The father and mother aspects of the divine consciousness, that have been forced apart, need to come back together now in the subtlest level of the heart, which is the natural balance point for every life form on this planet.

For most people born in England, who want to achieve that rare but necessary degree of heartfulness, there are two chakras to link up and balance: the throat chakra that utilises the mental thought-forms of the air element, and the base chakra which draws up the much-needed energies from inner Earth.

Without balance, we will continue to be hampered by the beliefs and priorities of some of humanity's spiritual slackers, in positions of power, with their fixed attitudes and hateful intentions. The subconscious mind can only bring forward an intelligent distillation of what it already knows but we each have a 'source self' that understands far more

Whether 2012 is the exact beginning of the Aquarian age or not is immaterial. The transformative energies are already enveloping the planet at a distance, available to those ready to engage and make use of them in service to the planet. We must rouse the courage to face the uncomfortable truths and ground them, so that, with a really concerted effort, we can access the subtle planes and breathe free again.

It is Summer and I am back in Glastonbury climbing the stairs to the Upper Room at the Chalice Well, to commune with my friend, Wellesley Tudor Pole. His deep wisdom is already impressing images of the past on my mind, mainly pictures of jousting and noblemen rescuing damsels in distress that I associate with the chivalrous Knights of the Round Table. I had previously pushed all this away as romantic tosh. Camelot was far earlier.

I can see a ritual circle, in a very early temple, with men and women alternately positioned, their minds focussed into an energy disc in front of them.

"There were four groups of twelve, each within its own energy sphere," Wellesley points out, "with a quartet of pivotal people representing Arthur, Guinevere, Merlin and Morgana, positioned at the centre, to balance each of these groups. That brings in the multiples of thirteen. Jesus, restrained by the mores of the time, had only men in his inner circle of followers. He had to find other ways to include the women."

The vast room, I am seeing, dissolves into a many-levelled, multi-dimensional reality. At the heart level, it is like the surface of a great pool stretching far to the horizon. There is no sense of separation, no limitation on the extent of its reach. The four groups are parts of one unified energy that enables them to be co-creators in the task of intricately weaving dual strands of consciousness into patterns that will manifest into form much later on.

The energy around the four pivotal people becomes crystal-like. They are communing with the great ones on the subtle levels and pooling their respective abilities.

This enables each of them to travel energetically to the many places and communities that support their mission, until there is a unified purpose spreading across the whole southwest of England.

"It is creatively interactive," Wellesley adds. "The six pairs in each group cover a full spectrum of capabilities, as in the zodiac."

Around each group, there is a powerful circle of spirit guides, with a small team from the angelic realms overseeing them all. They are not attached to any fixed form or experience or outcome. The four 'middle ways' intersect in the centre. Around each, there are spirals and other energy formations, drawing all layers of this group interaction into an intricate pattern.

"I was exploring these ancient influences during those dark days of war," Wellesley continues. "My group participated far beyond the concentrated sphere of energy in our own temple space because it had no bounds in reality. We worked with the essence of the trees and extended our influence into the realms occupied by those who inhabit inner Earth. We could be here, there and anywhere simultaneously, which strengthened our ability to turn the grim tide of events, and so can you, in the challenging work that lies ahead for you."

I still have many imperfections to overcome before I will be a completely integrated being who can stand firm in the face of this kind of karma-shattering endeavour. "I don't function very well alone," I confide to him.

"Few can, and Arthur needed Merlin much more than he realised. Within each individual and in all couples who link up in the various kinds of co-operative endeavour, there is always a karmic component, an inevitable flaw. Think of the Lancelot figure who undermined that particular experiment, and Judas who sent Jesus to his fate. It is small wonder that, in the greater scheme of human affairs today, it is almost impossible to find unanimity - but all such imperfection, too, is an illusion when we are ready to accept that."

He then suggests that I link Glastonbury to London.

"You already have a power point there."

"Yes, the heart chakra in the Coram Fields near Helios."

"Good. Now locate the other chakras, from the crown in the South to the base chakra in the North. See each as a round table. Identify the four elements and extend them up into a pyramid of energy, as in the great Giza edifice. Relate this to the Arthurian initiative and the astrological patterns, four elements with three signs relating to each, blended into a workable whole."

I know that this kind of unification is still ahead of its time, but this chat with Wellesley is launching a new burst of activity in my quest to explore the structure of the English identity as it struggles to reach a more subtle level of expression. For all of us in the Peacemakers Circle, next year will be one of intense activity.

❦

To effectively integrate my own sphere of light and dark energy, I am releasing a lot of my impatient earth karma, as is my colleague, Robin, whose channelling abilities are beginning to flower impressively. Like Maisie, when people come to us for aid, he brings through their past lives, so that I can help them resolve their issues and move on.

The subtle senses provide an accurate impression of the divine purpose that links us all. Properly motivated, they enable the spirit teams, working with us, to achieve much of lasting value. Above all, when I surrender to the heart, my mind stops revelling in separation and knows itself to be a fully functioning expression of the divine, which doesn't need to prove anything. The Aquarian age has arrived, and I need to pull all the fragments of my life together.

Recently, I have been besieged by many disquieting memories about the end of Atlantis but, now, I am accessing information from right at the beginning when the energy was being transferred here from Lemuria.

In those days, the senior priests could engage with high spiritual energies without losing contact with the deep primal places within Mother Earth.

Lemuria ended with major earth upheavals decimating what remained of the communities there. Most of those remaining in Perth had moved to Uluru in the dead heart of Australia. In Chile, there had already been quite a rapid reduction in the numbers incarnating. When the shock waves came from the central islands, they fled north and established what became the Inca civilisation. By the time of the final tumultuous earth changes, the area was unpopulated.

Those wishing to transfer the energies to Atlantis had incarnated in India. A former life of mine is very excited as he comes close to tell me his story. The Lemurian civilisation had not fully succeeded because of their excessive control but, in this first life of ours in the Northern hemisphere, he was concerned that any sudden liberation from the Lemurian constraints could lead to the pendulum swinging to the other extreme, when there would be a lack of discipline, focus and, especially, grounding.

He foresaw a battle between the light and the shadow and when he announced that, "for a time, the shadow will win", his seership was dismissed as deluded. He was right, though. Understanding the dichotomy between the two hemispheres was crucial to the success of the coming Atlantean venture. Major shifts in perspective and application still had to be grappled with.

My guide, Johosephat, steps in to tell me that the move on from the Lemurian energies was like a transition from a feminine energy to a masculine. It was a major disruption, but there was no mass migration. It was progressively implemented over a long period with quite small groups moving away from India to establish a network of communities, that would eventually form the extensive Atlantean civilisation, in what are now, Egypt, Morocco, Gibraltar, Portugal and the Canary Islands.

Over time, tens of thousands of people made the trek westwards.

A group of three extended families went directly to Rome where they experienced an early influx of the Christ energies and did not participate in the development of Atlantis at all. They had, in a sense, gone ahead of their evolution which, as later events unfolded, was not a wise move.

Each group of migrants included at least two of the more advanced people with telepathic abilities, who would pass on what is happening to those left behind.

My former life stayed in India because he felt they still needed to face the unresolved matter of how authority should be handled but, when the Lemurian experiment came to a complete standstill, he and his extended family were forced to join two other families who were about to make the arduous trek to the Morocco settlement.

There, the level of spiritual power was not what he was used to, and his concerns about authority were well justified. It all felt somewhat disorganised. There had been no priesthood established at first because the numbers were quite small, less than a hundred initially. It was never more than a thousand.

They had created and worked with fixed energy constructions without any actual physical buildings, unsure of how long they would be there. Their individual gifts were not integrated well. In a sense, everyone was a priest and everyone a teacher. Though no one was excluded, they had difficulty including newcomers according to their capability.

The three families stayed there for almost a year, wishing they could move elsewhere. My former life was determined to get to the main settlement, northwest of Fuerteventura, but he fell ill and, after experiencing painful body convulsions, died.

My next life, I am being told, was in a community near what is now Gibraltar, but no further information is forthcoming. My third Atlantean incarnation was meant to be lived entirely in the Portuguese jurisdiction but he didn't stay there. Being mega-assertive, he was determined to be near the spiritually advanced members and part of the decision-making process. However, on arriving there, he was assigned to a minor support role which didn't please him at all.

Moving forward to my fourth Atlantean life, which was again in the Morocco area, now known as Mentis. It had become the main trading post for the entire Atlantean region. There is a fully functioning priesthood, numbering 100 out of the 800 in the community and equally divided between male and female.

Only the most evolved are chosen to become priests. They know that if their priesthood grows too big, the overall tone will be lowered and this would sap their energies when doing the more intricate practices. The rest are allowed to participate in any minor rituals that were appropriate to their abilities.

They do understand that it is essential to keep an effective social balance with each member seeking to fulfil their evolutionary potential on all levels and in every area of their lives. Then, the individual harmony, balance and wholeness, that they establish, can be shared more widely.

The senior priests are still aware that their activities and abilities are vital to extending the achievements of the Lemurian period but they confined this to the Mentis area. Everyone, outside the priesthood, shares in the philosophy and develops many of the abilities, such as telepathy, that are useful in their more mundane practical lives.

They have little contact with the small island to the south. The advanced community there is still overseeing the network of small communities so that the entire energy structure of the Atlantean project can be kept intact

This life of mine does travel there to be ordained into the priesthood in a special initiation ceremony that opens him up to the deeper purpose of the Atlantean mission. I am registering this very strongly as he returns to Mentis to share his experience with his colleagues.

His understanding is quite advanced, particularly in the area of healing. He is not involved with genetic manipulation, this time, or in in the ways to produce heat and electricity using specific geometric shapes.

He does use both sound and light to cure disease and crystal energy in psychic surgery. His special skill is to emit certain healing frequencies from within the structure of his body and, by using various musical implements, he can produce sounds, so clear and sharp, that they can break through any resistance.

Inner guidance tells him how to handle the different levels of emotion which positively affect the chemical structure of the body.

During this 200-year high period, about ten and a half thousand years ago, they were finely attuned to the planet's evolution but, as in all things cyclic, the power began to recede. When the divine intelligence is ignored and we believe we can impose our own power, it is downhill all the way. This is what happened in the succeeding Atlantean generations.

૭

2013

The high Atlantean power was still dutifully dispensed to the Giza region via the small desolate island of Comino. The Giza community was well aware of the problems that Atlantis was experiencing in terms of hierarchy. So, rather than having a coterie of all-powerful high priests, they developed a fairly representative system of small groups instead, based on respecting collective decision-making and social cohesion.

Syrian timeline

Virgo began	Lemuria established	12,938BC	India/Australia/Chile
Mid Virgo	Height of Lemuria	11,863	
Virgo-Leo	Lemuria to Atlantis	10,788	Canaries/Morocco/Azores
Mid Leo	Peak of Atlantis	9,713	
Leo-Cancer		8,638	
Mid Cancer	Atlantis fell /Egypt began	7,563	Malta to Giza
Cancer-Gemini		6,488	
Mid Gemini		5,413	Great Pyramid built
	The first pre-Dynastic rulers at Hierakoupolis move away		
Gemini-Taurus		4,338	
Mid Taurus		3,263	
1st Dynasty	Menes	3,050	Abydos
2nd Dynasty			Abydos, then Memphis
	Power moved to Minoa	2,700	Knossos near Crete.
3rd Dynasty		2,686	Memphis
4th Dynasty - Sueferu		2,613	Giza
	Khufu/Cheops	2,589	Great pyramid restored
5th – 8th Dynasties		2,498	Memphis
Taurus-Aries		2,188	
9th & 10th Dynasty		2,160	Heracleoplis
11th Dynasty		2,134	Thebes
12th & 13th Dynasties		1,991	Itj-Tawy
14th Dynasty		1,782	Delta
15th Dynasty		1,650	Avaris
16th – 18th Dynasty		1,650	Thebes
	Power Minoa to Greece	1,525	Athens
	Akhenaten	1,430	Tel el Amarna
	Horemheb	1,319	Thebes
19th Dynasty	Ramses 1	1,292	Thebes
	Ramses 2	1,279	Thebes
20th Dynasty		1,186	
Mid Aries		1,113	Athens
Aries-Pisces	Power goes to Italy	38BC	Rome
Mid Pisces		937AD	
Pisces-Aquarius		2,012	
Mid Aquarius		3,087	Completing the Sirian mission

They were a self-sufficient community of equals, no more than 400. Communities being established in the Aquarian age could well emulate them. As with Atlantis at its height, women were still full members of the senior priesthood, though not quite as many.

Their considerable knowledge and ritual use of energy kept them at distance from the clans around them. They were respected for the peacefulness of their social structure and were not involved in any inter-tribe rivalries.

They had an effective telepathic connection with the Comino community and felt no urgency or danger coming to them as the end time grew near. They were secure and energetically protected because they understood that they did not need to unbalance themselves to keep their high energy in place, as the main Atlantean hierarchy had started doing,

The high priest on the central Atlantean island did allow in flashes of true inner guidance, alerting him to what was coming. He accepted his responsibility to manage this now inevitable event in the most harmonious way possible. Unfortunately, he did not fully understand the extreme imbalance that had been allowed to take hold. The intensity of the build-up of karmic energy prevented them from holding the power in place, with sufficient precision, to delay or minimise the upheavals that were about to sink their land in that most dramatic way.

At Giza, they were still accessing energy from their own local power source which was sufficient to keep their well-disciplined spiritual work going, without too much interruption. However, they were no longer able to support the 12 main satellite communities in the wider middle eastern area, right round to the Nubian province in Africa. Gradually, the moral authority of these satellites became debased and isolated.

The high priests at Giza had registered the oncoming devastation much more clearly than the priests at the Fuerteventura settlement, especially the timeframe.

They had accepted that the mantle would pass to them and were not pleased when, in the last months, some senior priests journeyed up to negotiate a migration.

The visitors saw themselves as the supreme representatives of Atlantis and expected to receive absolute compliance from this outpost. However, the senior Giza priesthood, at that time six women and eight men, was a far more balanced collective than they expected.

They were treated well enough but were firmly rebuffed when trying to take control as they had intended. Most significantly, the Giza priests did not alert them to how quickly they felt the final decline would happen because they definitely didn't want a band of ungrounded 'know alls' returning to take over, at any time. In a sense, they were sent back to their deaths.

13

The Atlantean Triangle

I return to Perth twice a year hoping to establish myself as a spiritual teacher while promoting my Nyaania charity to everyone I meet. As much as I find the give-it-a-go Australian energy immensely refreshing after the stuck English attitudes, Australia is not one of the more spiritually advanced countries on the planet.

Life is simple there. The people are open and direct but they are denying their wider responsibilities, particularly to resolve the racial issues still festering in their midst. To work on this karma, I am sharing a home with two aboriginal members of the Morrison family, Della, a fine singer and political activist, and her son, Kobi. He is one of only six people there who are assisting me with my Earth energy work.

I join their activist group and go on protest marches noisily denouncing the lawmakers who refuse to accept their responsibilities as custodians of this ancient land. I listen to many platitudinous Perth politicos who are completely failing to address the issue that Aboriginal people make up 5% of the state's population but 43% of the prison inmates. Juveniles are 52 times more likely to be imprisoned than their white peers.

It is easy to admire their energy but I feel that they lack the courage to step out of their victim mode and demand genuine equality. So, the old disempowering ways of privilege and corruption continue to cruelly dismiss them.

A generous community involvement and belief in a higher purpose are essential parts of the healthy human spirit. Where these are missing, there can only be a sense of betrayal. My beloved Australia has become proud for all the wrong reasons. There is a wilful blindness to the race issues in that 'lucky country' that goes back to the early colonial days.

Spiritual centres need to be established near ancient power points and, if possible, I want my Nyaania Community to have links with one of the more accessible Aboriginal massacre sites that remain scarred and weeping. I visit many of them with two very dedicated aboriginal elders. We successfully clear and harmonise the energies there but this now has to be carried on by younger members of their community.

I envision a time when there will be many groups linking up to empower an ever-expanding network that will bring about a substantial uplift to the spirit in this country – but clearly, not yet.

I have done much preparatory work but two months a year in Perth is not nearly enough to get the whole project moving. I am always optimistic and full of enthusiasm but though I meet many people who accept my vision, to a degree, I am not finding any who want to engage with the deeper elements in the national psyche and the karma involved, that would enable this kind of spiritual venture to put down lasting roots.

Most people want their spiritual growth to be comfortable but it is often a painful process to hear and heed the voice of the secret self. There are no easy ways to cast off the dependency and self-centredness that remain entrenched in the collective human psyche. When challenged, many, who ask me for help, soon become frightened and defensive, cynical even, and very confused

To achieve the freedom of an awakened spiritual consciousness requires us to focus into the heart and, from there, powerfully direct the grounded energies into a constructive future.

༺

Before dropping off to sleep, my mind often travels to the planet orbiting Sirius C, my true home. I had always viewed the inhabitants there as being noble advanced beings but, of course, I was one of them and I am certainly not that. This time, they do not seem to be physical in quite the way we are, and nor is the planet itself.

Beside me is the final life that I had there, at the end of the period after the fall of Atlantis when I wasn't incarnating on Earth at all. He lives at the base of a marvellous mountain that he is showing to me now.

He tells me that, even though he had extricated himself from the magical straight-jacket inflicted on him by his Libyan tormentors, he felt that he had been away from Earth for too long. He had adjusted his evolution to his home planet and it took a lot of persuading before he agreed to the Egyptian life that began a further round of incarnations here.

Johosephat comes in to elaborate. "It is time you learnt more about why your efforts here on earth are so resisted." He has my complete attention.

"The most unbalanced part of the Sirian thinking was the belief that the northern hemisphere was the progressive, spiritually superior part of the planet. They used the southern hemisphere for their mining and slave labour."

"They also drew power from above in their rituals, believing that their Sirian Sun was where the divine resided and their planet, and all life forms on it, were subservient to this omnipotent being. Not all that different from how it has developed on Earth but a little more extreme."

"The Lemurian migrants realised this and kept very near to the main Earth power points. They knew that their main purpose was to strengthen their part of the southern hemisphere that had become energetically dissipated and unbalanced. They, only gradually, expanded their contact with local people and they kept away from emigrants from other planets when first moving into the Atlantean phase."

The Sirians were not the only advanced civilisation to come here from other planets. The Pleiadians are one notch below them in evolution and started their sojourn on this planet in China. They didn't come in spaceships but travelled here on the inner planes where time is not such an issue, and then directly into incarnation. Some initially had controlling intentions, but most came to learn and assist.

The Egyptians focussed on the Orion star cluster but Johosephat assures me that the Pleiades is more important. "They tend not to be very expansive and certainly have none of the world domination agenda shown by some intergalactic visitors. They are much more heart orientated and, over many centuries, have worked in tandem with the Sirians, often preparing the way for the major initiatives, notably in establishing the Minoan civilisation as a set of integrated communities each with their individual areas of creative expertise."

The Minoans emphasised beautiful architecture with lavish architraves which they filled with exquisite ornaments. That kind of artistic endeavour is the Pleiadian's strongest asset which was most evident, in Italy, during the Renaissance. This was their finest achievement. They later drew in Michelangelo and Leonardo da Vinci who were both Sirians.

"Many spirits incarnated from Sirius over this long period, often many times." This is at least my 32nd incarnation. I'm a slow learner.

"Some, who incarnated here at the beginning, didn't continue, and others came in later. Perhaps a quarter of those still active in this project are incarnate at this present time."

Our main task is to, at last, put aside thoughts of superiority and learn the ways of individual, collective and planetary balance, so that we will attain and express the profound spiritual abilities of the Atlantean masters and pass their lost truths on to all those willing to listen. Yes, but do we have time?

"Too many former Sirians, in positions of power, still believe they are superior to what they see as lesser mortals and their dominant egos are continuing to unbalance the planet in very serious ways. They abused power many times, leading up to the Atlantean debacle and then, later, in Egypt, Rome and, eventually, everywhere."

The real nightmare situations usually stem from very small numbers of ego-based people and their followers whipping up widespread mayhem involving masses of innocent people.

I am registering that George Bush, father & son, were the most recent Sirian expats in the White House. Obama is a former Pleiadian and Trump, I would imagine, came from an unstable planet far away.

෴

After investigating the Roman karma in London, the Peacemakers circle moves on to the Tower of London to better understand the subsequent Norman influence and how it further unbalanced the energy of this country towards a quite ruthless authoritarian control.

William the Conqueror started standardising England's feudal rules in their favour in the Domesday Book of 1086. The brutal and widespread sequestering of land enabled them to control everything that remained of the English heritage and a former life of mine did his best to stop it happening. This control has never been properly challenged since then and, today, 6,000 individuals still own 50 percent of rural land.

The class system here, which keeps everyone in their allotted place, is effectively built into the genetics of the populace with many present lives of the earlier ruling class still dominating the English political system today.

The members of each of the Royal houses over the centuries have come from different planets. Sirians step forward when there is an important task to carry out. I am looking for clues as to when they were on the throne. Everything points to the Tudor times. Although the Roman army had left many centuries before, significant influence from there continued via the Roman Catholic Church. This link needed to be severed.

I was always sceptical that the King Arthur story is actually a part of the Sirian initiative, but I am coming around to this view now that I have learnt that the Tudor royalty were convinced that they were descended from him.

Henry VIII became increasingly paranoid later in his reign when he sentenced an exceptionally large number of people to imprisonment in the Tower of London. Over 70,000 were executed overall, mainly by beheading. The Royal axeman probably still has a lot of karma to work out from that.

Queen Elizabeth I continued to represent the symbolic presence of Arthurian lore in renaissance politics. In 1570, the Pope branded her illegitimate and, five years later, she visited Kenilworth Castle, where an Arthurian costume party and masque were being held, to put paid to that heresy. Upon her arrival, she was met by a woman dressed as Morgan le Fay who greeted her as Arthur's heir.

Even today, both Prince Charles and Prince William have middle names that include Arthur. There is a story going around that the present royal family originally came from a planet where reptiles were the dominant race, an interesting concept - and 'why not?' More important to this book is my belief that, when the Windsor dynasty has run its course, the Sirians will step in again to lead the country forward with a full people-based programme.

2014

I have spent many years exploring the course of the Atlantean energy through the dominant cultures from Egypt onwards but there is much more to discover about the power that came from Atlantis into Wales where it was taken up by the Druids who met the Roman advance head-on.

To start with, we must confirm the three points of the Atlantean triangle that had been in place during the whole Atlantean period, up to the time of its destruction?

The first is the pivotal point on Fuerteventura where the earth energies, going up, are meant to be precisely balanced with the sky energies, coming down. However, later on, the priests there began to emphasise the reaching up, causing their balance point to rise higher and higher up. This meant that their link with the second triangle point near Mentis, where the upthrust energy is emphasised, was strong and productive, while their link to the third triangle point, where the power is directed down, was gradually neglected.

The advanced priests, on the central island within the triangle, were aware of what was going wrong but their attempts to balance what was happening at the extremities were only partially successful. The Mentis high priests eventually did not link up with this third triangle point, and the community there, at all. This meant that the energies they were directing through Comino to the Giza region were becoming increasingly elevated. An envoy was sent to Mentis, to address this, but he was ignored by the priests who believed they knew better.

Then the especially wise main priest on the central Atlantean island died suddenly, followed by another senior figure, soon after, which meant that those overseeing the Atlantean project were now unable to keep the integrity of the whole triangle fully intact.

So, where exactly is the third triangle point?

As always, we rely on a map to guide us. We firm up the Fuerteventura/Morocco link, but the other point is...at first, elusive. We attune more precisely and wait. Suddenly, Robin's finger shoots across an area in the Azores, which I immediately experience as spiralling downwards. His finger is correct, this was where the earth-orientated Atlantean power was generated.

This is similar to the original Lemurian triangle with an obtuse angle that reflects the extent of the imbalance in their energy which they had brought with them from their former planetary home.

When the end time for Atlantis was fast approaching, many priests had become especially open and unprotected on the everyday human level. This cut them off from the community around them. On Fuerteventura, they were entirely unaware of the burgeoning shadow culture growing up within their field of influence. Self-appointed shamans, in many outlying communities, were experimenting with debased practices including black magic.

They became cocooned in a spiritual bubble, unable to ground themselves. Their unbalanced leaders were oblivious to the physical catastrophe that they were drawing to themselves, from deep within the earth, until it could not be reversed.

Everything sent out is fully responded to, so their spiritual arrogance inevitably self-destructed their civilisation. They were living above themselves, and could no longer see the wholeness of what they were trying to create. Indeed, they were unable to manifest their spiritual dimension on Earth at all.

Fortunately, the self-contained earth-orientated community in the Azores was more resilient than those at Fuerteventura and Mentis.

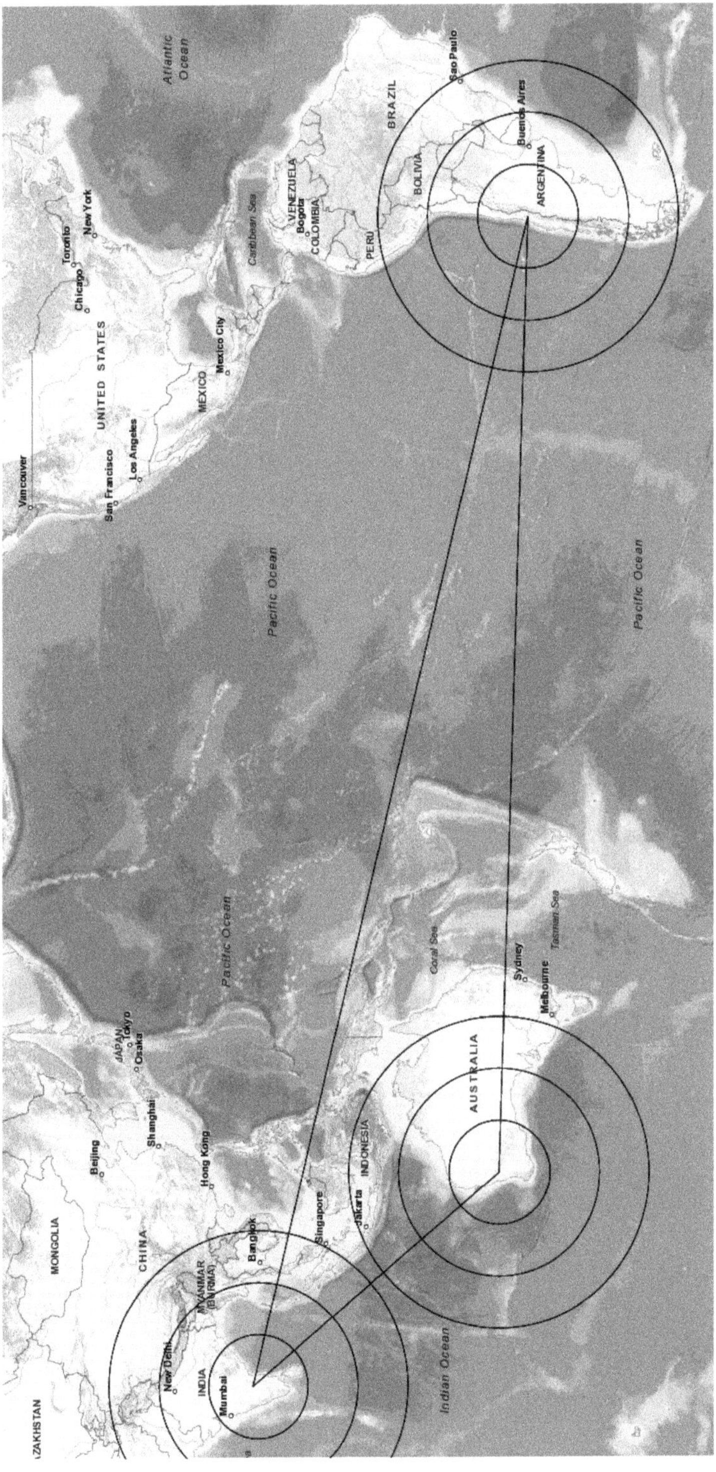
Atlantic Ocean
New York
Toronto
Chicago
UNITED STATES
Vancouver
San Francisco
Los Angeles
MEXICO
Mexico City
Caribbean Sea
VENEZUELA
Bogota
COLOMBIA
PERU
BRAZIL
BOLIVIA
Sao Paulo
Buenos Aires
ARGENTINA
Pacific Ocean
Pacific Ocean
Pacific Ocean
Coral Sea
Tasman Sea
Sydney
Melbourne
AUSTRALIA
INDONESIA
Jakarta
Singapore
Bangkok
Hong Kong
Shanghai
Beijing
JAPAN
Tokyo
Osaka
MONGOLIA
CHINA
MYANMAR (BURMA)
New Delhi
INDIA
Mumbai
Indian Ocean

14

Leaving Lemuria

2015

My astrological chart informs me that this is a good year for travel but I have to coerce Robin into flying to Perth with me. Although he incarnated in Astroeth at the beginning of the Lemurian civilisation, he has never come to this particular spot, choosing instead a second life at Uluru, the enormous and sacred red sandstone rock formation in Australia's dead heart.

Robin accepts that our visit will help to re-awaken this ancient land. He is willing to support me because he knows what a special place it is on my spiritual journey. At first, though, he is ill at ease with the energies and does not seem to appreciate the places I take him to.

That is, until we attend a lecture by a visiting aboriginal barrister who is fronting a legal campaign for indigenous land rights where I have my first sighting of a dragon. It rises from the earth in front of him, huge, reddish-brown and surprisingly benign. Afterwards, he tells me that he takes this dragon wherever he goes.

"There are many people who would like to see me dead", he confides. "My dragon keeps me safe."

"Perhaps I could have a dragon for myself to help with the Earth energy work I do?", but he cautions me. "They are not pets. Working with dragon energy is very spiritually demanding. If you approach them with wrong motives, they will singe your soul."

I tune into the elemental dragon energies when Robin and I go to the Darlington area, which contains the highest expression of Solar-plexus energy in the entire country. It also supports the awakening of many other power points up and down the West coast.

Several friends are keen to accompany us but we must do this alone. When awakening the primal past, only those strong enough to work with this kind of power should do so. Without training, it is difficult to put ego concerns to one side enough to cope with the intensity of what is being uncovered. It could be disastrous for their physical and mental equilibrium.

We are surrounded by a circle of the early Lemurian priests as we probe into the concentrated energies lying deep in the earth. I have met them before.

They are joined by a group of 12 aboriginal elders who also encircle us, but much closer in. Their tribe tended this powerful area at the time of the first settlement. They are very aware of the karma inflicted on the land by the early white settlers and how important their stewardship of this crucial energy is for its long-delayed outworking. These elders promise to stay close to us and guide our path for the remainder of our trip.

Many aboriginal people living in Perth today had native blood in a former life. They need to allow the great ancient ways to be expressed through them, once again, but in a quite a different fashion. In another life, many of them were the early settlers who did so much harm. They have chosen to be on the receiving end now, to rectify what they set into motion. That is why many indigenous people are bitter and confused. They believe they should be white.

We accompany these elders to the ceremonial area overlooking those rocks on the other side of the Nyaania Creek. What did they do when they realised that the coming of the colonial settlers would lead to the rape of their land? There was only one way to protect their tribal heritage. They sealed it off.

Without access to it today, the Aboriginal people are cut off from the deeper resonances of their far back past. One of the Elders in spirit bemoans that very few of the young aboriginals in Perth are opening up to what they wish to tell them.

We look across to this power centre with great reverence before asking the custodians to admit us. They agree, provided we do not awaken any more than the surface earth energies. Many over-enthusiastic seekers, visiting here, are drawing on the power without knowing how to use it. They are grasping after things far off in their evolution and could do severe damage to their destiny flow. They could even delay the profound re-awakening that is coming, though they cannot prevent it.

Nothing pure or deep can be accessed that is not in keeping with the spiritual needs of this ancient energy source. Even Robin and I can only approach to a limited degree. This is certainly not work for spiritual dilettantes who fantasize about higher realms.

I know that I am often over-zealous. This trip is forcing me to look at that tendency more closely. Past karma can exert a tremendous pressure when approaching these sites from a purely mental perspective. We must focus precisely into the deeper reaches of our hearts to access the inner realms of pure intention and guided implementation.

After crossing the Nyaania Creek, we stride up onto those ceremonial rocks where we notice some houses up the hill overlooking the site. Many of the occupants are probably unaware that they are guardians of the area. One chap is certainly trying to take the power for himself. We strengthen the natural protective shield around the rocks to prevent this from continuing. When I sit quietly on my own, dragons come immediately to mind.

I am aware of the two cultural traditions: the European folk dragons and the Chinese river-serpent dragons that command the benevolent forces of nature, the rain, rivers, lakes, and seas.

Since the Middle Ages, European dragons have been depicted as huge lizards with scaly or feathered bodies and an exceptionally long tail. They live in underground lairs and direct fire from their mouths when opposed.

The Christian Church appropriated elements of the old pagan legends, linking many of them to Satan. The monstrous dragon killed by a Christian hero such as Saint George may have symbolised a suppressed pagan cult.

Sitting quietly on this ceremonial rock, I am determined to contact one of these fascinating elemental creatures. My first attempt confirms that entry into the dragon realms can only be bridged through faith.

I focus attention into my heart, then more deeply. I seem to be in a gloomy and claustrophobic cave but, when I relax more, the walls start to sparkle, as though crystals are embedded in them.

Then, I feel a presence beside me. "Don't look round," it says, with a soft, reassuring voice. "If you try to see me, you will probably project a form from deep within your consciousness that I do not actually have. We have been misrepresented for centuries, based on the wild imaginings of superstitious people who glimpsed us as grotesque creatures, etheric imprints carried forward in the global psyche since the days of the dinosaurs."

It is impossible to cast off my childhood dragon images, so I don't look. It feels as though my new acquaintance is projecting no form at all. He seems intangible, yet very present.

"Still your mind. We are relating telepathically. Share my reality. See with my eyes, and I will show you the world that I help create. I exist in a parallel universe to your own and I have never incarnated into physical form. In your world of the four elements, you create opposites in a confrontational way. We have only three elements and are effective only when working in threes. One takes the lead, the other two remain supportive and balancing."

He invites me on a journey of the mind around the area that he is responsible for developing energetically. I am eager for this, knowing that he will hold me safely within the confines of his awareness.

"It is a matter of being fixed and free, both at the same time, on adjacent levels of consciousness. Your evolved humans, such as the Buddha, functioned in that way but it is rare in your world now."

"We operate always with that kind of freedom. Everything here is fluid. Our thought energy moves spontaneously in currents and waves, weaving forms and patterns which are entirely integrated but we are not usually aware of them as we work. This skill keeps quite complex structures of energy intact while allowing everything to move freely within them."

"I am an air dragon known as Alcos. My wings are actually energy forms that help me to manoeuvre my mind spatially. Do not be one of those who fear releasing their very limited reality. Let go and be who you really are. Are you ready to fly with me?"

I grunt an affirmative.

"Subdue your imagination and let my mind blend with yours. Have no expectations. Hold this focus but, at the same time, let go and trust me. Then your mind will soar."

Suddenly, I am able to register a great number of things simultaneously. Yet, there is a very strong central focus within me that isn't shifting at all. I am following streams of consciousness that are weaving in and around each other. We encounter one energy form that is whirling like a tornado. I must get right inside it. Another is pulsating and we are forced away.

Eventually, I am drawn back to the 'cave', which I now experience as a spherical space, largely without substance.

What had thrilled me was merely a job of work for Alcos. He assures me that, "it is never dull because it takes only an instant in Earth time and requires very precise involvement. There is no chance for the mind to wander."

"So, you three dragons are actually one?", I guess.

"Most certainly", is the emphatic reply. "In our more

complete state, we are able to commune with our guides and inspirers from the inner levels. It is very satisfying."

"In the human experience, you are denied full contact with the subtle planes, so you often feel isolated, unaware that our world is only a thought away."

"Does evil exist here?", I ask.

"Oh yes, there are obstructive dragons existing just outside of our consciousness, always watchful for a chance to get in. We don't relate to them directly. That only feeds their sense of importance. They are masters of deception, so we establish and maintain an integrity that is usually immune to attack."

"If we were to drop our guard or choose to engage them in battle, then we would be vulnerable. You become what you oppose. Some of the disturbed energies you encountered, when you travelled with me, were the shadow ones trying to intrude. And some of the fiercest currents were a result of what is happening above ground."

"Though we have very little useful contact with your human world, the trees, are very involved with what we do. Having a more subtle consciousness and with their roots beneath the Earth's surface, they can maintain a much more intimate involvement with us."

"Next time, I will introduce you to my two partners if you decide to work with us." I wish him a grateful goodbye.

Will I take up his generous invitation? What would such a commitment entail? Complete faith, for one thing. If you doubt yourself in this work, you can't continue. Do I have the necessary discipline to hold the balance and the ability to handle the unknown with a clear mind and from a stable foundation?

I do urge caution to those thinking of contacting dragon consciousness. Today, many people open up to spiritual energies and are carried along by influences that encourage an unrealistic view or are held back by old belief structures that no longer serve them.

Many approach the subtle worlds for what they can get

out of them and are caught up in fantasy perspectives from earlier times, that constant repetition has reinforced. Dragons are not extravagant beings. They navigate the realms of inner Earth from a precisely focussed centre, moving easily to where they are needed.

The scramble to be spiritually elevated, allows desire and glamour to take over, preventing progress. Elaborate belief structures have been created, based on nothing real, where bigger is believed to be better, where higher is seen as superior to the lower. We need to understand that every expansion of consciousness must be surrendered to our Source Self, so that the soul can truly breathe.

The Aquarian age needs completely new concepts, deeper understanding and updated images of the benevolent life forms who share this planet with us, so that we can learn to engage with them usefully. We must start with a clean slate, or the past will continue to impose itself on the present, carrying forward all the misguided elements.

During that initial journey, I was able to turn myself upside down and enter into the dark places as confidently as I could into the regions of light. I send a thought to Alcos to assure him that I will certainly join him on another journey soon.

A few days later, I take Robin to the base chakra site, located inside the doctor's domain, again without him noticing. I make contact with my old mentor who still chooses to remain nameless. He gives me some fresh teaching,

"From time to time on your earth, there are opportunities for the far back past and the far-away future to come together and, in this meeting, a surge of transformative power grips the imaginations of those ready to engage with it."

"You and many others are preparing the way for the eventual widespread dissemination of this new range of power. When the network of orientation points on the etheric level is complete, they will link up to the physical.

From within it, a surging, pulsating, cauldron of energy will erupt and a new kind of world will be born – but you will not be alive to see that. "

He then points firmly to a map on the screen in front of him. His finger arcs the coast south of Perth and I know, without being told, that I must go there.

"Is this where the main points on the Lemurian triangle are located?", I demand. Then, more excitedly, "Is that where I had my first life on the planet?" but the wily old man has retreated.

Robin and I pore over the physical map for hours, plus some googling, moving across towards Albany before settling on a site near Young's Siding. We agree, "This is certainly where the local Lemurian triangle is situated."

It is easy to enthuse my Aboriginal friend, Eddie, to drive us down to visit "many secret places where wondrous beings live." Our spirit inspirers are still revealing no more to us. So, we three intrepid explorers set off with a very unclear itinerary.

Although most parts of Australia are barren, the south coast is green and fertile. We pass through the lush vineyards of Margaret River and the tall trees in the "Valley of the Giants."

Here Robin and I become aware of the great deva who looks after the area. Devas are elemental beings with all four elements active. More evolved than the dragons with three. This one has a massive auric range, able to embrace and nurture the entire natural world we are passing through. The fertility of the area is largely due to the presence of this impressive being and those who support him.

Our inspirers have alerted us to a disused rubbish dump near Young's Siding. The local storekeeper directs us down Lake Saide Road, straight to it. The google map overview showed dozens of rocks in close formation, but we are surprised at how huge they are.

There is one that attracts me, the most powerful in the cluster. I sense that it is very close to where I was born in my first life on the planet. It is hard to relate the enormity of what I am experiencing. I sit with my back to it. My family and neighbours are there all around me, third and fourth generation immigrants from that planet far away, dressed rather like the puritans. There is a tremendous community bond between us.

I expect the atmosphere to be peaceful but all of them have strong opinions which they are thought projecting at each other. They use a very formally structured language which I assume they brought with them. I am being held by my mother.

Moving forward to the adult years of that first life of mine. He has developed an especially dogmatic, "This is how it has to be", all or nothing, no compromises, approach to life but he does have a sense of humour, fortunately, that kicks in when the many disagreements, he has with those in charge, become too intense. However, when engaged in their rituals and group channelling, he allows himself to blend closely with them.

Because they have no past earth lives to support them from the spirit realms, their most recent lives on the planet orbiting Sirius C are inspiring them from the subtle realms.

Connecting into the rock, in present time, I sense that a non-physical energy generator, linking back to the Sirian planet, is still there. It is being overseen by two spirit beings. Those early settlers followed the instructions coming from there, in their rituals and when they directed energy into matter. Technology was used to produce bountiful crops and generate heating and lighting naturally. This link will be needed again when the Sirian project gets closer to completion. The beginning and the end must become one.

The colony here is quite small, mainly scientists and their families. Farming communities have been established elsewhere and there is an educational facility at a site above Newman Beach. It is a kind of university campus where the astronomers and the horticulturalists, both male and female, teach the younger ones in their charge. I must visit there.

The south coast of Western Australia is a wonder place to observe the stars. As I stand, open-hearted, with the vastness of the sea in front of me, I harness the energy that comes from it. My soul is opening to greater possibilities and, as I ground this, my spirit flies.

For light relief, we visit a haunted lighthouse, mindful of the fact that people like their spooky places. It is probably mean of us to remove the intruder but we do it anyway.

We are also drawn to an impressive rock that stretches right down a massive cliff to the waves crashing onto it. Again, it is awash with exhilarating energy, but troubled.

Large rocks possess an individual consciousness that can be related to and this one needs a lot of comforting. Many people visit here without awareness and the mind inside the rock is not altogether happy with this. "I have work to do," it complains. "These people only want to take my power for themselves. They don't ever help at all."

As I look towards the bay, a large imposing Neptune-like figure rises up from the waves. He isn't very happy, either. "If they don't work with us then we hold back the rain. There are many droughts, these days, and they only have themselves to blame."

What can I say in response? "Sorry about that, mate," seems a bit inadequate. I send him some heart support anyway.

We make our lives so much more difficult when we interfere with nature or just pay no heed to the vital inter-relatedness within it. Clearly, this is set to worsen over the coming years if we don't accept our responsibilities very soon.

15

The Beast of Bodmin Moor
2016

I am rather chuffed at having connected back to my first life on Earth and made an active mental link with my life on the planet surrounding Sirius C. However, my restless nature is saying that I must explore further forward again when I return to London.

I often wonder what happened to the power that was in the Azores. Robin is trying to tune in to the Azorian priests but they aren't responding.

The Fuerteventuran priesthood had only wanted to support them to make contact with the subtle realms when they knew that, from their triangle point, they needed to reach down into the heavy planetary energies and create structures there that would be useful to the spirit beings supporting them.

"Well," a voice interjects, "we did try to please the Canary crowd at first, but we soon realised that they were leading us astray. It is true that we did not extend the energy very far out to the surrounding areas, which they believed we should be doing. They saw us as effectively inactive and gradually withdrew their support."

"We did eventually send sent a group of 200 priests north to England when we became aware that the destruction of our civilisation was fast approaching. A further band of 400 refugees followed, some years later, to escape the waters threatening to flood our land. These 600 were the forerunners of the Druids."

"Wait, just a minute," I interject, frantically trying to fit this stunning revelation into what I had discovered about the west country during our early trips to Glastonbury, and subsequently.

He continues anyway. "We will direct you to an important site on Bodmin Moor in Cornwall where we will carry this understanding forward with you."

ے

In late June, seven of the ten members of the Peacemakers circle take off in two cars heading towards Bodmin and our motel.

From there, we head north to our chosen site on the high East Moor, a wide-open expanse surrounded by far away hills. I have never felt power as other-worldly as this. It feels almost like a separate universe. Elation expands me as the sky lights up and the hills seem to retreat further, slowly at first then at an accelerating rate, till infinity is just a breath away. It would be easy to lose one's identity here. I have certainly been here before in the far distant past.

Staying focussed in the heart is the only way to remain present and, at the same time, be in touch with the Druidic realms within the earth. We establish our usual Peacemakers sphere between two large sentinel rocks. My inner sight opens up as I go down into the earth where the Druid workers are waiting for us. One is standing in the foreground, surrounded by light.

Using my usual peripheral perception, I can see him drawing the energy of many colours into himself as he approaches. He seems to stop on both sides of me. I draw him into a unified focus directly in front of me. I can hardly believe it. It is the old man from my childhood bedroom, my teacher and protector. But here?

"You're Merlin," I cry out, "the wizard and master of the inner worlds I have come to meet?"

"One of them," is his unforeseen response. He pauses while I take this in. Of course, the original Merlin has had many incarnations since.

"This is how it works for we sorcerers, my son. Allow the power to flow in now, with all the rainbow hues, and register the many sounds of eternity as they replenish your reserves. You already know you are far more than human, a multi-dimensioned being. You restrict yourself far too much."

Of course, I know that. He asks me to focus back to when I was his apprentice. Was I? Memories flood in and my doubts fade away. Yes, I believe I was.

"Think transmutation, not only of matter but of souls. We were remnants of the authentic Atlantean priesthood dedicated to keeping the deepest links with the earth alive. While not a shamanic culture, we kept our heritage even when we lost the exact form of our beginnings and much of the magic remained with us."

My mind is struggling to assimilate his revelations. When was this? Not when the Arthur gang visited Bodmin and connected up with the Merlin crowd at the time of Camelot. Before that, certainly. Over the preceding centuries, many of the Arthurs had resolutely kept away from their Merlin counterparts, which widened the gulf between them. Probing further, I place this life several hundred years before the Romans came.

He confirms this. "We were already making very strong efforts to extend the Druid energy out to influence the rest of the country and even Europe, and we were very successful. After that, there was a time of consolidation before a much greater expansion was meant to take place. In this life, my Arthur counterpart needed to conserve energy and link up communities within the triangle."

"Triangle?" I interrupt.

"Yes, there is always a triangle. Don't expect me to tell you more than that," he chortles. "Arthur wasn't doing the kingly thing that time. He was learning to manage families and communities well. It was a slow period of growth for him in his attempts to create stability and, as I hoped, he based himself within the Glastonbury circle.

This gave me the chance to slip into Cadbury and secretly establish my presence and purpose there. We had no communication at all. That schism was vital."

He goes on to tell me that I was one of his alchemy students, a subject that has always fascinated me. A telepathic link developed between us which I must now develop further. The bond between us grew to where he trusted me enough to make me his envoy to Bodmin. I was instructed to set up a magical Druidic operation there.

He continues, "I didn't actually envisage the Romans coming but I knew something destructive was on the way which would inevitably block the flow of energy if I did not send it underground. I wanted the space, within the triangle, to be an oasis of power and protection for the British Isles. We were not entirely successful, as you know, but it left an imprint on the land that you are beginning to register."

I ask where the latest Merlin is incarnate at this time but he rebukes me. "Isn't one of us enough at a time?"

Then, proceeding patiently, "You may think that the coming of the Roman armies and the almost total destruction of our culture was the end of our influence. We could have walked away when on the spirit side, and some did, but enough of us remained close to continue with the work."

"It is nearing the time for the rebirth of the Druidic culture in a new form, backed by the pure Atlantean energies adapted to your modern world, but humanity still has some decades to go before it will be ready for this renaissance. Your involvement will help my colleagues and I gain a greater flexibility in what we can achieve."

With his help, I seem to be drawing the centre of the earth towards me till it is just inches below my feet. I am aware of a dark speck at the centre of my heart which I must enter into now.

All that happened in this special part of the moor is now available to me. Members of farming families, from that time, are crowding around. They are still protecting and developing this small pivotal area within the vastness of the Druidic orbit.

I look around our Peacemakers circle, each immersed in making contact with the inner earth in their own way. We are a team doing the same thing but from entirely different perspectives.

Several register an eerie atmosphere that they feel is trying to invade us. Perhaps it is the infamous 'Beast of Bodmin', a mental construct that keeps intruders and many of the locals away. I am pleased that none of us are finding this energy too much to handle. It could easily disturb psychic people, venturing into the area, who are not grounded enough.

I wander over to one of the large rocks and, place both hands on it. I am aware that the well-integrated Druid community are still linked up here within a clear geometric pattern.

Merlin continues, "All sites have an active and an inactive phase, each with a different potency and ability to influence the surrounding areas. So, there was a succession of expansions and contractions in the energy here. The Romans attacked at a time when the power had already retreated."

He tells me that the Merlin, incarnate at that crucial time, responded to the clear warnings of what was to come and sealed off the power from intrusion. He arranged for the Bodmin families to merge with other communities further South in Cornwall but also one in North Devon, more shamanic in nature, where they used the natural energies creatively but did not ground them much. These two groups linked up through emissaries. This kept a continuing Druid presence in the area that the Romans were entirely unaware of.

"However, the Arthur energy areas across the country were not nearly as well protected. Centuries later, there was a pressing need to bring the Arthur and Merlin initiatives together, in the so-called Camelot, before the connection was completely lost. It didn't succeed very well which is why you have been called in with a mission to assist with this very important re-emergence and reunification."

We return to our cars and drive as far as we can towards an outlying settlement on the high moor, where we feel the massacre happened. Those living there at the time were refugees from a threatened village nearby and not active members of the Druid priesthood.

We hike across the vast moorland to a somewhat desolate place where we feel the disturbed energy has been held, following those dreadful events. It is very contained, so as not to intrude on or disrupt the main power source on the East moor. We try to make contact with those continuing to work on the karmic energy there but, initially, there is no one around to greet us, only a great sadness.

I realise that these people had lived a number of lives working in these outlying Druid fields over the centuries. They were regulars on the scene, before being called upon to act as unwitting martyrs to keep the Roman forces away from the more important sites. We need to free them from their restraints.

My Merlin stands right back when a group of these trapped souls approaches us. They are held almost motionless as we take them back to those earlier times. We are aware of the screams, the pain and the cruel enjoyment that the Roman soldiers felt as they hacked these villagers to death.

We remain detached so that we can facilitate their release. Much of their surface pain had already been worked out over the centuries, but the part that it played in blocking the subsequent English spiritual development has remained immense. Frustrated energies have been rising up from the earth around us like lava from a volcano.

Bringing release to these stranded ones was certainly the most important achievement of this trip. There are a lot of very relieved spirit friends approaching to express their gratitude.

After this, we journey over to nearby Camelford, the main location of the late 6th century Camelot, to help bring the two strains of Druidic expression, harshly severed by the ancient Romans, back into alignment.

Of course, the Rome-orientated Christians added another layer of illusion to the proceedings which we have no intention of investigating. What you don't arouse, you don't have to deal with.

"Their suppression of the Earth Mother is for others to work on," my Merlin confirms. "You can't do everything."

Further investigation of the Camelot story is for a later trip but snippets are coming through as we go down a small gulley to a creek near Slaughterbridge, said to be the location of Arthur's last battle against his arch-rival, Mordred.

"Don't believe everything you read," Merlin asserts, "He is one of my staunchest allies."

That night, we stop at a haunted Inn just outside of Glastonbury. I am planning the forward link to London when a reprimand comes, "Link back to Bodmin as well. Strengthen that side of the triangle, as your former life did, all those centuries ago."

ॐ

Our Druid friends accompany us back to London and into the debating chamber in parliament. They can only get really close to the physical dimension by using earth people able to ground them.

After setting our Peacemakers sphere in place, I sit my Merlin down in Jeremy Corbyn's seat knowing his influence will be of some help in the debates. He seems very comfortable there. Jeremy was obviously a Druid in a past life and Theresa May, a high-up Roman officer who was responsible for his death during the Anglesey massacre.

Our attempts to chip at the tight crust of privilege surrounding many senior politicians are being very strongly resisted by spirits, maybe their own past lives, who will do anything to sustain and reinforce their tight and often cruel structures of power on both sides of the veil. Their austerity dogma rewards the rich and is leaving many needy people, around the country, suffering as a result.

These selfish individuals in charge are largely ignorant of the spiritual laws underpinning true leadership. They do not understand that their actions are not only karmically destructive to themselves but are counter-productive to their objectives in the long term.

To tackle the old entrenched energies in the English psyche, we need to stay entirely detached and non-judgemental, otherwise, we will inevitably hit an equal and opposite force head-on. Everything must be carried out from the centre of our energy sphere. They cannot get at us there.

16

The Arthur ~ Merlin triangle
2018

We have established that the two linked evolutionary streams of the English character were split into the Arthur, throat-based orientation, based in the Glastonbury area, and the earth-orientated Merlin energy that we encountered on Bodmin Moor. Our next task is to find the third triangle point where they initiated their structure of power and developed a unified purpose that was eventually directed further afield. This could only be in Wales - but where exactly?

Tanya, a long-time member of the Peacemakers, has a fascination with ancient yew trees. With lifespans of up to 4,000 years, they are the venerable representatives of the tree kingdom in this country and are found in many of the oldest churches. Yews have witnessed some of the pivotal happenings in our history. It was under a yew that the Magna Carta was sealed and the same yew was believed to be a secret meeting place for Anne Boleyn and Henry VIII.

Her investigation leads to the "bleeding yew", located in a churchyard in Nevern, a Pembrokeshire coastal town. We all agree that this is certainly where the Druid ancestry originated. A trip is immediately arranged.

Five of us travel to Bodmin Moor where we head for the triangle corner point on the East Moor, situated between two stone outcrops. Again, we energetically extend our reach to the surrounding hills, a considerable distance away.

The archaeologists tell us that 10,000 years ago in the Mesolithic period, hunter/gatherers wandered this, then wooded area - and during the Neolithic era, from about 4,500 to 2,300 BC, people began clearing trees and farming the land. At that time, various megalithic monuments were built.

From the Bronze Age that followed, 200 settlements, with enclosures and field patterns, have been discovered, while there are many prehistoric stone barrows, long cairns and stone circles scattered across the moor, none of which attract us. We are there to explore the main Druid settlements.

Bodmin draws on energy from the whole of Cornwall. After dutifully tuning in, we delve further into the reasons why the Camelot experiment needed to happen. The two streams of Druidic development, reasonably integrated in the early days, had become separated when one of the Arthurs decided that he had to be King, ordained by God, with sole responsibility for much more than his part of the story. When he cemented his authority and moved his operation to Cadbury, others who thought they should be 'top dog' were immensely annoyed, including an early incarnation of Lancelot.

The well-integrated Merlin tribe had settled in Bodmin where they maintained a strong inner connection with the advanced Atlanteans in the spirit world. Many of their attempts to establish a balanced society of equals were wonderfully successful, for a short time. Their exploits formed some of the earlier layers of the Camelot story.

Here, on Bodmin, we are aware of the six entirely self-sufficient families whose settlements were arranged in a geometric pattern. The honest, heartfelt connection between them meant that their cooperative way of living was deeply entwined within the land and it spoke to the far future.

Of course, the circumstances are not conducive for such societies to last. All around, the other tribes are warring with each other and they are caught, quite defenceless, within that. Yet they are heeding the call to do it anyway.

By the 6th Century, with the Druidic presence destroyed by the Roman armies, Celtic Christianity is encroaching on the area, with the Roman version of absolute Papal authority close behind. There needs to be a more concerted attempt to unify the Arthur and Merlin dynasties.

There is little they can do to prevent the religious takeover but, on the inner levels, a merging is needed to set an integrated purpose for the entire country in place, which will be reactivated at a later time. In other words, it is necessary to re-establish an older, more democratic version of spirituality in the ethers around Bodmin before the Atlantean heritage is entirely suppressed there.

Imagine King Arthur's round table of twelve men and twelve women linked up with the Merlin round table of twelve men and twelve women; and feel how powerful their achievements together on the inner levels would have been. This is the essence of the Camelot mission.

In the various myths, Arthur's knights are all named, but apart from the much-maligned Mordred and Morgana, most of Merlin's earth-orientated people are not individually identified. The glamorous, but unbalanced, Arthur clansmen have dominated the story right through to the present time, preventing a truthful picture.

However, a schism came about, not only between the two factions but also between the men and women within them. The serious male/female imbalance, that Arthur encouraged, is one of the main reasons why Camelot failed.

My mind is now following the Druid story that led up to it. From the beginning, the two most advanced members of the original 200 earth-based Azorian immigrants, one male, one female, were recognised as their undisputed leaders and this continued over time.

Arthur's 'knights', however, had been leaders and high priests at the time of the early Nevern settlement and now harboured ego-driven ambitions to replace him. Although the Camelot Arthur is descended from the first one, there were a number of interlopers who stepped in, along the way, determined to be the clan leader. This usually led to open conflicts.

The later incarnations of the first Merlin are always incarnate for the most important ventures and they have kept the balance very effectively at Bodmin. I am now tuning in to the Camelot Merlin at his home on the East moor waiting for the aggressive, forward-thrusting Arthur to come to him. The King has heard about this wise old man from the locals and is being inwardly encouraged to submit to his tutelage. Only then would his wayward, fantasy-driven throat energy, creeping ever upwards, be brought back into a more balanced alignment.

This doesn't go to plan when the two men meet. Sensing the threat to his authority, Arthur is in no mood to give up any of his power. He resents having to kowtow to an old fool speaking philosophical flimflam about equality and storms out. He does not return.

The next phase of our trip requires us to contact the Camelot triangle around Bodmin, still active on subtle levels. Robin picks out the three apex points; the first is near the road leading past Dozemary pool leading up to the infamous Jamaica Inn. We park our car and I feel drawn to a point over the ridge where some very lively upthrusting energy is thrusting up but the others convince me to settle for a more stable, less energetically exciting spot near the road. A simple orientation is all that is required, then on to the second point at Killibury Castle.

This 'Castle' occupies the summit of a low hill in the rolling coastal belt between the River Camel estuary and Bodmin Moor with gentle slopes on all sides, dropping to the River Allen on the south-eastern side.

Excavations, beyond the protected area of the monument, revealed extensive structural features and occupation artefacts from the later Bronze and Iron Ages. There is evidence of re-occupation in the post-Roman period at the end of the sixth century. Ah, Camelot again.

On approaching, little of this is evident. Shrubs and half-mown grass obscure any obvious features. After forming our circle, we become aware of fighting and aggression, in the atmosphere, that needs clearing.

A very angry local chieftain speaks through Robin. He tells us that he and his clan had been happily settled in the area for a long time when a very imposing headman from a way off came in, hoping to link up his area with this one. This chieftain had wanted things to go on without any changes and did not warm to the idea, but he invited the visiting leader over anyway.

He did not expect this man to be accompanied by a group of his warriors, and when the discussion was clearly not going to his guest's liking, he was surrounded and brutally killed. His main allies in the clan suffered the same fate and this fierce intruder had no difficulty in taking over the whole region.

This is an early attempt to get those supporting the Arthur line to blend harmoniously with the, more earthy, Merlin contingent. This Arthur substitute failed totally. He introduced karmic energies into the area that made the subsequent Camelot mission much more difficult.

ॐ

The following day, we look for the third triangle point at Slaughterbridge near Camelford which we had visited previously. When we can't locate it initially, we pay to look around the 20-acre Arthurian Centre where the masculine and feminine energies urgently need to be more precisely balanced.

There, we come across the 'King Arthur Stone', dating from 1602, but it had lain on the river bank for a thousand years before that. This coincides with Arthur's final battle with Mordred which brought the fellowship of the Round Table to an end. The earliest stories place the battle of Camlann at AD542 but Camelot, I believe, began some decades later.

The fierce battle turned the small river, red with the blood of slain men, culminating when Arthur and Mordred fought a hand-to-hand combat across the bridge. Arthur slew Mordred but he had already received a fatal wound from Mordred's poisoned sword, and soon staggered to his death. Mordred is always portrayed as representing evil and is, in some stories, the illegitimate son of Arthur and his half-sister Morgan le Fay.

The stone carries a Latin inscription and rare Ogam, an ancient Celtic script that indicates there were Southern Irish people in North Cornwall at this time.

From there, we spot the area we are seeking on the other side of the stream. It is usually a soggy area but, on this occasion, it has dried up in the heat, leaving awkward ankle-twisting terrain. We form our usual circle and attune to the energy. The triangle is complete.

On our way to Nevern, we stop and make contact with the central point of our main Cadbury/Bodmin/Nevern triangle which is out to sea.

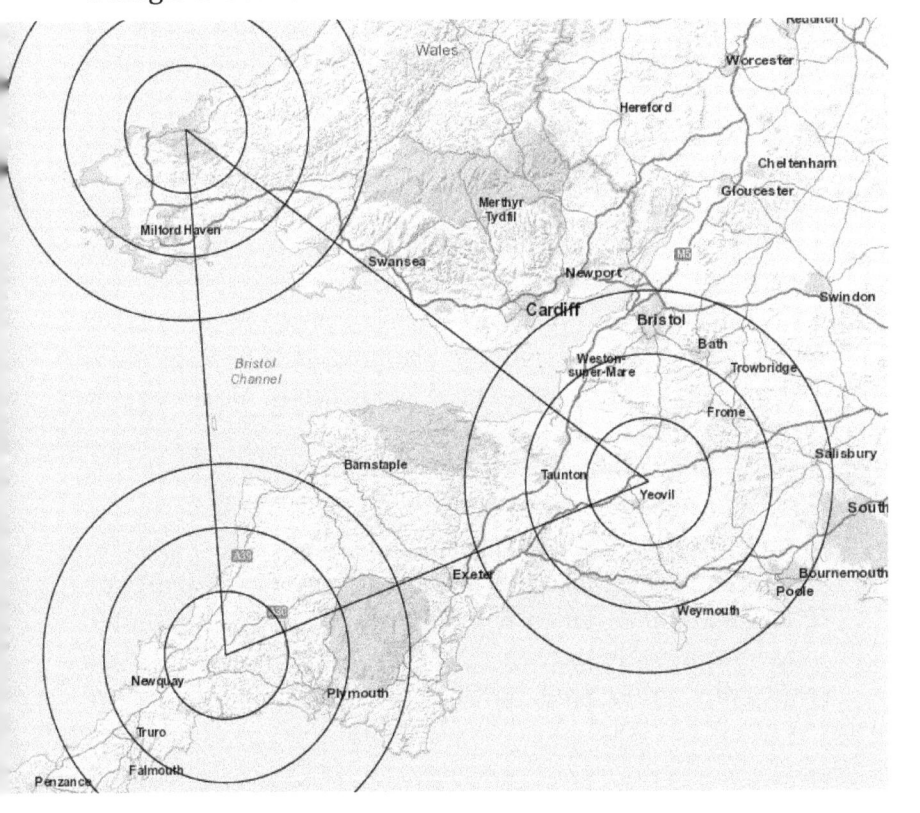

On reaching Nevern, we visit the church and, on opening the gate, the "bleeding yew confronts us, bleeding profusely. A 12th-century Norman church was originally built on the site but only the tower remains; the rest being from the 14th century through to 1864 when restoration took place. The nave has a stone vaulted roof.

We hold our usual meditation inside, and I feel inspired to draw the Christian power towards me before banishing it dramatically from the building, like in an exorcism. I am shocked at the aggression coming up in me and the elation that follows. The Church was built almost on top of the power point, instead of at a distance from it, and this inhibited the natural energies which we are liberating now.

We then visit the castle on the hill 150m northwest of the church. Little remains, though we learn from a woman excavating nearby that it was built around 1108 by Robert fitz Martin as the original Norman headquarters in the Marcher lordship of Cemais.

We sit down to meditate. Robin transports us back to the time, around 10,000 years ago, when the destruction of the Atlantean civilisation is anticipated and the first group of 200 are sent 1450 miles from the Azores to the safe beaches of what is now Newport.

Chosen for their pioneering spirit, they are the most grounded and subtly attuned members of their community. It is a very smooth transition. Merlin is one of them.

Being an earth-orientated contingent, they adapt easily to the forest environment and relate intimately to the creatures that live there, especially the pixies, gnomes and elves who help them transmute the quite disparate energies found beneath the earth. They are contained and comfortable in their new surroundings and they are especially influenced by the more advanced elemental beings who support them in their magic.

There are the horticulturalists who create food forms that suit and nourish their human needs and the medicine men & women who distil herbs into complex natural remedies, so that each patient gets exactly what is needed, with no serious side effects.

Because these Azorian migrants embody very restrained and stable energies, with none of the expansionist tendencies of their counterparts in the Canary Islands, they fit in nicely with the local communities they encounter, in the many valleys away from the coast where water is plentiful and life is harmonious.

These tribes co-exist peacefully, never encroaching on the lands of their neighbours, and they are not threatened by these unexpected arrivals, who seem friendly enough. They are mystified that the newcomers are able to settle in the area near the coast where they believe the spirits of the land are based.

The dual nature of the overall English temperament requires a precise balance and so, the second wave of 400 Azorians dutifully take on the very mental Arthurian air element, distancing themselves from the earlier migration to form a quite separate and distinct clan.

They are the intellectual hub of this Atlantean continuation: the scientific minds, both male and female; the mathematicians and specialists in geometric forms; the energy architects who can focus thought so precisely that a roof can be laid on the walls of a temple with such exceptional precision that the rain and cold winds are entirely repelled. They also set the subtle energies in place that frame their rituals.

The former Azorian lives, of both groups, visit in their spirit forms and participate in the ceremonies. This ensures a strong connection to their shared former heritage where both the air and earth elements were directed downwards. To proceed, they must create and stabilise their own varieties of elemental power strongly in the present time or a divergence in their mutual objectives could develop that will be difficult to rectify.

They all have telepathic abilities. However, the more earth-orientated souls are the realists, adept at accessing the past and seeing into the future in practical ways. They hold their more expansive, idealistic, air-orientated brethren in check, preventing them from taking their evolutionary impulses too far and too fast for the entire population to assimilate.

Over time, these two groups manage to simplify and adapt their Atlantean skills enough to teach some of the other communities in the vicinity, with only very practical lifestyles, the ways to keep the elements out and how to contact their ancestors directly.

Many generations follow before they have completely adapted their Atlantean past into the very different Druidic form. Indeed, it is two thousand years before they send out emissary groups to visit and then infiltrate themselves into the more progressive communities further afield, teaching them some of the esoteric and magical skills they still have.

They have already made contact with these other communities on the inner planes and extended the evolutionary impulse to them, so that when their descendants eventually arrive in physical form, they are easily able to relate to these less evolved people.

Interesting though this is, I am here to track Merlin down. On venturing beyond the far end of the castle into some low-hanging trees, I am suddenly teetering on the edge of a drop down into the gully below. Stepping back, I look for a way to climb down. The others aren't so keen. Fortunately, the column of power extending up from the source, down there, is wide enough to include where we are standing. I start my attunement, looking down, but I soon realise that, to receive the full potency, it is necessary to focus into the heart and look straight ahead.

As I soak up this marvellous natural energy, I am transported, back in time, to a secluded spot down there where a ritual is taking place. The original Merlin, with an incredibly powerful aura surrounding him, is kneeling in reverence towards a cliff face a short distance away. Suddenly, a presence rises out of the earth in front of him, not a physical form, more like churning lava.

My inspirers tell me that he is an advanced entity from the inner planes who has never incarnated in human form. This concentration of slowly pulsating energy is causing a spiralling surge to come up into me. My heart feels connected and a bit scared. Can I handle such a forceful experience?

Is it a deva spirit, or from another dimension I know nothing about? I can't tell. This exceptionally powerful energy is becoming more solid as it enters the physical realm.

Merlin appears unaffected by the intensity being generated. He looks up at this spirit towering over him, which seems to be taking on a human-like form. Though profoundly fascinated by this, I am far from ready to engage with such a challenging presence. I turn away and break the link.

One of my inspirers tells me that this very dynamic link between Merlin and his non-human mentor continued through many subsequent incarnations, including the crucial Camelot one.

We return to the church, where we learn that, while the Merlin community occupied the Nevern area, the much larger Arthur clan located their main ritual centre on the nearby Dinas Island which we proceed to visit. On top is a farmed plateau which signs tell us not to encroach on. A naughty part of me wants to leap over the fence and race to the top of the hill waving my arms in defiance, but I restrain myself.

A track around the outside enables us to reach the major energy point on the far promontory. It was a long way and the climb is testing my old body to the limit. I invite the original Arthur to join us in our circle but he pays no heed.

The Atlanteans were adept at using such places and knew how to draw these subterranean energies into their rituals. This involved balancing the light and dark forces as they contacted the inner plane replicas of the ritual buildings they had left behind in the Azores. Initially, they were only able to establish them as energy structures, but gradually they managed to re-create the old physical forms in their new environment.

These temples were, in a sense, satellites of the old and trusted places of communion with other realms and distant places in the universe. Their lives were dual-focussed and their spirit guardians lived with them almost as if they were physical.

I now have a very clear overview of the full Sirian mission, having tracked the flow of events from the Lemurian beginnings until the Atlantean period when it split. The sky-orientated evolutionary stream flowed from Morocco to Egypt and then across Europe to England where it met, and crushed, the earth-based steam coming from the Azores.

So, the linking up was prevented and humanity has taken an inordinately long time to address the imbalance inherited from the Sirian planet. There are few leaders anywhere who are not too high up energetically and convinced that they are superior to the planet on which they walk.

We are nearing the end of our King Arthur tour which certainly has left me with much to ponder on how this new understanding will assist the work we need to do in London.

Druids are all around, congratulating us on our achievements. We are continuing what they started and they are eager to accompany us back to London where they will enjoy themselves in parliament with their mischievous sense of humour. Even the most hidebound backbenchers and brexiteers will be unable to withstand the full force of their heart energy.

"Bring on Boris", one Druid chappie chortles in my ear. "We need even greater instability in those august chambers before sanity can be invited back in. He's just the man for the job."

They tell me that he was a barbaric Viking plunderer, in an early life, determined to squash the Celtic spirit that was rising up and seeking freedom. He especially despised the Druidic traditions then.

It wasn't guilt that kept him away from England after that. There were many other European countries for him to Lord it over and he was a member of an aristocracy in many of those subsequent lives. In Spain, he was a member of the Royal family. There was not one balancing life as a pauper.

During a privileged life in Normandy, at the time of William the Conqueror, he turned his attention back to England where he had his next life as a rich landowner in a provincial city, with a great sense of entitlement, who did not treat his serfs well.

In a later life, he was Thomas Lancaster, the eldest son Edmund Crouchback and Blanche of Artois, Queen Dowager of Navarre. On reaching the age of maturity, he became the hereditary Sheriff of Lancashire and really loved the aristocratic lifestyle. He often imagined himself having absolute power in parliament.

He served in the coronation of his cousin, the weak and divisive King Edward II, in 1308, carrying Curtana, the sword of Edward the Confessor. Lancaster had openly supported Edward, but he gradually switched his allegiance as the conflict with dissident nobles wore on,

Lancaster particularly despised the royal favourite, Piers Gaveston, who mocked him as "the Fiddler". His private army helped separate the King and Gaveston. He was one of the "judges" who convicted Gaveston and saw him executed.

In 1321, Lancaster headed a rebellion of dissident barons against the crown and was defeated at the Battle of Boroughbridge. He was taken prisoner and, at his trial, was not allowed to speak in his defence. After being convicted of treason, he was beheaded near Pontefract Castle.

His continued presence there as Boris J only makes the Peacemakers more determined to deal with the cruel trespass into the English soul by former invaders from Europe, now establishment figures, who need to be dragged, stage by reluctant stage, into the present moment.

Many Whitehall mandarins have karma that requires them to dismantle the systems of establishment control that their former lives set up. This is the main outcome that the Aquarian Age is meant to achieve in this country.

On our way back to London, we decide to stop off at Cadbury Castle to seal the Druid triangle in place, so that its influence can spread widely across the country. We skirt Glastonbury town, not wanting to be caught up in the familiar distractions there, staying again at the Old Pound Inn. After a good night's sleep and an over-generous breakfast, we set off to that multivallate hillfort that we last visited in 1979 when Maisie channelled Uther Pendragon.

We Peacemakers are very ordinary people, quietly working away as a team. This is essential to developing the stable structure of energy that our spirit guides need. Each member provides continuity and adds a special creative gift, such as colour, sound or crystal healing ability to the mix. This enables the patterns of energy beneath the surface of the earth to be identified and worked with. We are all determined to see new ways of social organisation coming into being for the benefit of all, along with a peace that lasts.

I am aware that we are helping to prepare for the coming phase when England must go through a very challenging heart-orientated purification in order to throw off her remaining imperial inclinations and class system. This is already progressing behind the scenes, and on other levels, to eventually establish a fully integrated and morally sound administration, working in the best interests of all people, an example to many communities to the east, still grappling with lesser motives.

There are many loyal Sirians in and around the British government to contact, and we will continue to enable our Druid friends to influence anyone in the adversarial parliamentary debating chambers who is willing and able to deal with the madness that has overtaken our political and economic structures.

The transformed spirit of Camelot is waiting to be enacted in parliament, with the latest Arthur as P.M, organising and inspiring a healing of all that went amiss over the centuries. Standing beside him will be his Guinevere, their noble principles engaging with the minds and hearts of committed parliamentarians who need to align themselves to the power of the Father Sun which they will then merge with the power brought up from the earth by a modern Merlin, sitting alongside his Morgana. All four will have equal authority but, of course, this unification will not be easy. There will be many willing to play the Lancelot role.

For England to become the leading moral authority in Europe, it will require the two Atlantean streams, from Rome and Nevern, to be merged into an effective co-operation. That sounds marvellous but, at the current speed of change, it will probably take between eighty and a hundred years before the English people will look back and say, "We have finally moved on."

It is impossible to fully communicate the immense peace that I am feeling now, standing beside my Peacemaker friends, on both sides of the veil, as we look out over this beautiful countryside, with its many secret hideaways yet to be discovered. I am filled with gratitude that, in this torturous quest for truth, I am never alone.

CHRONOLOGY

The overall Sirian mission is scheduled to reach its zenith at the mid-point of this Aquarian age. Taking 2012 as the start, this will be around 3087AD. After that, other planetary groups will gradually take over and the Sirians can return to their home planet, job done. What a relief that will be.

2012	The beginning of Aquarian age
2119	England is the dominant moral influence in the region
2226	The power and responsibility returns to Italy
2334	Then Greece
2441	and Minoa
2548	By then, the Egyptian karma will have been worked through
2656	Back to the Atlantis triangle, Morocco, the Azores & Fuerteventura
2763	The central Atlantean position will be stabilised
2871	Then Lemuria – Perth, Santiago and India Linking in to the special American involvement which includes Hawaii
2978	Global consolidation
3087	The peak of the Sirian mission. We can soon go home.